FIRST LOVE
THAT LASTS

by

Bob Buchan

Unless otherwise specified, all quotations are from the New American
Standard Bible (NASB).
Other Versions include:
TLB — The Living Bible
RSV — Revised Standard Version

I.S.B.N. 0-914903-25-X

For Worldwide Distribution
Destiny Image Publishers
P.O. Box 351
Shippensburg, PA 17257

"Speaking to the purposes of God for this generation."
Printed in U.S.A.

ACKNOWLEDGMENTS

Many people have prayed for me, encouraged me, and assisted me in the production of this book. Special thanks go to Jan Seabaugh, Lauren McEleney, Mary Evans, Barry and Patti Keene, Mike Baird, and Lloyd Hildebrand, for their help in the editorial process.

Words cannot express my appreciation for my parents who have supported me throughout the years and have played a major role in making this book a reality. I am especially indebted to my mother, who has been a faithful typist and editor; and to my brother, Jim, who has blessed my Christian life in so many ways and who provided me with many valuable insights. I am also grateful to my wonderful wife, Linda, and our three children, who have stood behind me with their love, prayers, and incredible patience.

Most of all, I give praise to my Lord Jesus Christ, for He is worthy of my highest devotion and the fruit of my life.

Cover Design
by
Mark Tracey
Illustrated Alaskan Moose, Inc.

TABLE OF CONTENTS
First Love That Lasts

Getting Off the Starting Block 1
Distorted Concepts 13
Guarding Your Heart
 (From the One Who Loves You Most) 25
Restoring Your Spiritual Youthfulness 35
Barrenness in Busyness 43
Burnout: The Disease of the Over-Committed 51
The Crippling Effects of Habituation 63
Unfulfilled Dreams 73
Digging Up the Roots of Bitterness 79
Hurting Christians 89
Your Christian Fellowship: Help or Hindrance? ... 95
Laying Aside Every Encumbrance 103
Sprinting to the Finish Line 115
Appendix A 123
Appendix B 125

ABOUT THE AUTHOR

Bob Buchan is currently serving as pastor (along with some dedicated colleagues) of Christian Community Church, a dynamic, Spirit-filled church in Columbus, Ohio. Prior to that, he served in full-time ministry in an evangelical United Methodist Church for three years. Since receiving Christ as his Lord and Savior in 1969, Bob has been blessed with some rich opportunities for growth through his involvement in Young Life, Campus Crusade for Christ, the Fellowship of Christian Athletes, and Overseas Crusades.

Bob's pastoral experience and extensive counseling training (M. Ed.) have provided the numerous case histories scattered throughout the book. The names have been changed and the stories modified slightly to uphold confidentiality.

I know your deeds and your toil and perseverance, and that you cannot endure evil men, and you put to the test those who call themselves apostles, and they are not, and you found them to be false;

and you have perseverance and have endured for My Name's sake, and have not grown weary.

But I have this against you, that YOU HAVE LEFT YOUR FIRST LOVE.

Rev. 2:2-4, NASB

INTRODUCTION

I had been feeling tired and distracted in church that Sunday morning, but as I stood up to sing the hymn, I felt a flash of pleasure. It was one of my old favorites, "My Jesus, I Love Thee," a song with a melody that is a joy to sing. As the organ played through the chorus, I cleared my throat and got ready, then felt a nudge in my heart to pay close attention to the words.

I had sung this hymn countless times in my life, but I had never really focused on the lyrics. While the rest of the congregation began to sing, I glanced over the verses:

> I will love Thee in life, I will love Thee in death,
> And praise Thee as long as Thou lendest me breath,
> And say when the death-dew lies cold on my brow,
> If ever I loved Thee, my Jesus, 'tis now![1]

And I thought, "Do I?" Could I honestly say I loved Jesus more now than ever before? My thoughts raced back to the days after I first met Him, days filled with excitement, answered prayers, zealous witnessing, and the powerful presence of God beside me. But could I say I had grown in my love for Him?

Many Christians who begin their lives with Christ with that same overflowing joy find that after several weeks or months, the excitement has worn off and the "spiritual goose-bumps" have vanished. It seems that relatively few can truthfully say that their love for Jesus is greater today than it was during those first, glowing days as Christians. Many of them wander away. Many of them do not find their way back. Entire churches have grown cold in comparison to their earlier dedication to the Lord.

The church in Ephesus had its beginnings on Paul's second missionary journey (50-52 AD) when he visited this city with Priscilla and Aquila. Later Paul spent about three years there, working to see the church solidly built. In Acts 19, we see the outbreak of a great revival in Ephesus with many people being saved, filled with the Spirit, healed, delivered from demonic oppression, and completely changed. Extraordinary miracles occurred, and the "word of the Lord was growing mightily and prevailing" (Acts 19:20). But this is the same church that is addressed approximately forty years later in the book of Revelation, and by then it had developed some real problems:

> I know your deeds and your toil and perseverance, and
> that you cannot endure evil men, and you put to the test
> those who call themselves apostles, and they are not, and
> you found them to be false;
> and you have perseverance and have endured for My
> Name's sake, and you have not grown weary.
> But I have this against you, that *you have left your first
> love* (Rev. 2:2-4).

The Ephesian Church had experienced a glorious beginning and had risen to prominence among first-century Christians. There were many commendable qualities in these believers: they were an active hard-working group of people; they persevered in the face of strong obstacles; they were intolerant of evil men, false apostles, and those who were distorting the gospel; and they had not grown weary following the Lord. (vss. 2, 3).

Nevertheless, God was not pleased with them because they had left their "first love." Commentators are divided over the real meaning of this passage. Some writers say that the "first love" was their original love for Jesus, which was waning in the midst of busyness and their emphasis on maintaining biblical orthodoxy. Other scholars believe it speaks of the former love these believers had for one another which had now been abandoned. A third opinion is that "first love" is a general term that applies to loving the whole of mankind and not just fellow Christians in particular. Rather than making these interpretations mutually exclusive, there is a good possibility that this passage refers to all three.

Although we cannot separate loving God from genuinely loving His people, Jesus clearly articulated what our *highest concern* should be. He tells us to love God supremely. This is the greatest pursuit in life!

Our Lord was asked by a Jewish scribe one day, "What commandment is foremost of all?"

Jesus answered by saying:

> The foremost is, "Hear, O Israel; The Lord our God is one Lord;
> And you shall love the Lord your God with all your heart, and with all your soul, and with all your mind, and with all your strength" (Mk. 12:29, 30).

Regardless of our particular understanding of the meaning of Revelation 2:4, the rest of the Bible leaves us with no doubt that our ultimate love and loyalty belong to God. Loving people is indeed critical to our Christian lives, but it can never be a substitute for making Him our first love. No one should be more important to us than the Lord!

Jesus Himself said it this way: "He who loves father or mother more than Me is not worthy of Me; and he who loves son or daughter more than Me is not worthy of Me" (Matt. 10:37). Our Lord couldn't have spoken in more graphic terms to describe the importance of our relationship with Him. He assumes we do love the members of our family, but He requires us to love Him even more.

The beautiful thing is that the more we love Jesus, the more love we will have to give. He is the author of love and shares it freely with us so that we might pass it on to those who cross our path. If, however, something short-circuits our relationship with the Lord, our capacity to love other people is diminished, and we fail to treat them as He intended.

This is evidently what happened to the church in Ephesus. They were diligent in doing good deeds and enduring in their Christian faith, yet God was not satisfied. Their original love was gone. Just being busy didn't impress Him. He wanted their hearts. He got their labor. It wasn't enough.

Has your life become a set of routines? Have you become overwhelmed with Christian activities — prayer meeting one evening, Bible study on another, plus two worship services on Sunday and a few committee meetings squeezed in here and there? What about your private devotional life? Are you experiencing quality time with God in worship, prayer and Bible study?

Although our spiritual walk may have gotten off to a good start, God is concerned about how we are doing today. We may be involved in essentially the same activities (going to church, attending prayer groups, etc.) as we were when Christ first came into our lives, yet find that they have lost their joy and meaning for us. Never stopping to question ourselves, we simply keep on working, clinging to the memory of how fruitful our works once were. Or, we may even begin to grow apathetic and uninterested in spiritual things, gradually pulling away from God and any meaningful church involvement. Anger, exhaustion, and exasperation then start to show up in our attitudes. The desire to draw close to God diminishes. Our first love begins to fade.

Even though there are many people who are struggling just to maintain the love for Jesus they once had, God's perspective is that we should *grow* in our love for Him daily. If we are focusing all our efforts on simply hanging on, we are bound to make little progress. Like the church at Ephesus, we will present to the Lord a second-class devotion, which satisfies neither Him nor ourselves.

Has your personal walk with the Lord been on the decline? Are you merely going through the motions of worship and prayer, with no genuine satisfaction in your heart? Does God seem remote from your life, a distant voice that no longer seems to apply to you? Do you think He has stopped speaking to you, leading you onward, and caring about your needs? Do your prayers seem to bounce off the ceiling?

Let us take a look at some of the reasons why so many Christians lose their former enthusiasm and become spiritually stale. Let us also consider God's solutions for each one of these reasons. Our Lord is in the business of renewal. He can reach out and touch the burned-out Christian, filling him all over again with fresh, exciting revelation. He can restore the old zeal and recreate the former vision. He can explode in our hearts with a powerful, sustaining love. One of the most wonderful things about God is that He *wants* to. He wants to make our love for Him new again.

What about you? Does God have your heart, or have you left your first love?

[1]William R. Featherstone and A. J. Gordon, "My Jesus, I Love Thee," *Worship in Song* (Kansas City, Mo.: Lillenas Publishing Co., 1972), p. 44.

1

GETTING OFF THE STARTING BLOCK

"Hi, my name is Bob," I said, introducing myself to a guy I'd never seen before in the school cafeteria. My friend, Robin, who was one of the few Christians I knew in our high school, invited him to join us for lunch. He accepted eagerly, seemingly excited that someone cared enough to reach out to him. He introduced himself as Dennis, and as we talked, it soon became obvious that he was starved for friendship.

Every day after that, Dennis would faithfully search for us in the lunchroom and sit with us. It was only a matter of time before our opportunity came to witness to him, and witness we did! Although Dennis came from a traditional church background, he didn't know what we were talking about when we spoke to him of having a personal relationship with Jesus. At first he appeared uncomfortable, changing the subject whenever he could, but we continued day after day to proclaim the word of God with "great zeal, power, and boldness." After all, since he kept hanging around us, we figured he must be interested!

It wasn't long before Dennis began to go with us to a Christian fellowship meeting on a semi-regular basis. Several months went by and, through our constant challenges, Dennis finally expressed a desire to receive Christ. While sitting with him in my parents' car, I seized the opportunity and rushed him through a "sinner's prayer" to invite Jesus into his life. In spite of my excitement, it seemed to be a rather emotionless, matter-of-fact experience for him. I prodded him and cued him, trying to get him to show some feeling over what had happened, and tried to assure him that he was now a brand-new creation in Christ and that all his sins were forgiven.

It was soon obvious to me that Dennis was displaying a shallowness in his understanding of the gospel, and I often saw him reverting back to some unbiblical concepts about Christianity that were left over from his childhood. "He needs to be discipled," I thought to myself. "If only Dennis would become more involved in a Bible-preaching church with a good youth program." Thoughts such as these churned around in my mind as I pondered how I could help him become more dedicated to Christ.

My efforts and suggestions didn't help much. There was an apparent roadblock in Dennis' walk with the Lord, and no amount of discipleship training, Bible teaching, or exhortation from myself and others was able to overcome it. Much to my dismay, I lost track of Dennis during the summer break. He stopped coming to our Christian fellowship meetings and all my efforts to reach him failed. I was worried about him — where would he be without *my* help? How could he possibly stand strong for Christ without being swept back into his old way of life?

When school resumed in the fall, I dreaded seeing Dennis, expecting to find him backslidden and unreachable. My fears were confirmed when I finally ran into him. Dennis was very uneasy around me and no longer wanted to talk about the Lord. We didn't meet for lunch any more, and I usually only saw him from a distance. Even though I continued to pray for him, my heart ached over his apparent apathy.

A few months later, Dennis strode up to me in the hall with a big grin and a whole new look about him. I will never forget the expression of joy on his face as he excitedly exclaimed, "Bob, you'll never guess what happened to me! Just the other day at work, I saw a pamphlet about Jesus and I picked it up and read it. The words came alive to me and I prayed to commit my life to Christ. Bob, I've been *born again!*"

As I stood there, amazed by Dennis' testimony, I couldn't help but think about the times Robin and I had shared the Scriptures with him. Although we had devoted hours and hours to explaining the gospel to him, he had never responded like this! I was perplexed by what he was saying. What had made this experience so different?

There was no doubt that Dennis had been profoundly changed. I had never seen him so eager to follow the Lord. No longer did he have to be coaxed to read the Bible and pray, or to go to church or to fellowship meetings. In the months that followed, an incredible improvement took place in his character and personal life. But I was confused. Hadn't Dennis already received Christ as his Lord when we prayed together in the car? Yet I had to admit that there was something about his more recent experience that was deeper and stronger than the first one. What was it?

As I thought about it, I remembered that, when I was fifteen, I prayed to receive Christ after being confronted with the gospel by a man who witnessed to me at the Ohio State Fair. Since I had only parroted the prayer in response to his urging, my life was not changed at all. My heart was detached from my mouth, and the words I spoke at his insistence had no real meaning to me. Within a few days, I had put the whole incident out of my mind.

Several months later, however, while watching a well-known evangelist on television, God touched my heart in a special way, leaving no doubt in my mind that I had met Jesus Christ. This time my life began to change in dramatic ways. God Himself revealed His love to me and showed me the sufficiency of the blood of Christ to secure my forgiveness. This encounter with Jesus was revolutionary, changing my life forever.

I realized then what it was that had made the difference in Dennis' life, and mine. God had brought us to a place where we recognized our need for Christ, and through His grace, He birthed in us a genuine desire to follow Him.

Who Do You Say That I Am?

Many people dismiss Jesus' claim to deity by accepting Him only as a prophet, a teacher, or an unusually wise man. Others deny that He existed at all, or worse, label Him as the reincarnation of some other prophet. This is not a problem of our generation alone. Even in Jesus' day there was confusion and uncertainty about who He really was.

Jesus confronted the issue with His disciples in Matthew 16:13-17:

> Now when Jesus came into the district of Caesarea Philippi, He began asking His disciples, saying, "Who do people say that the Son of Man is?"
>
> And they said, "Some say John the Baptist; and others, Elijah; but still others, Jeremiah, or one of the prophets."
>
> He said to them, "But who do you say that I am?"
>
> And Simon Peter answered and said, "Thou art the Christ, the Son of the Living God."
>
> And Jesus answered and said to him, "Blessed are you, Simon Barjona, because *flesh and blood did not reveal this to you, but My Father who is in heaven.*"

Our Lord challenged His disciples with perhaps the greatest question in all of life: "But who do you say that I am?" Jesus was not concerned with what society as a whole was saying about Him — He wanted to know what His disciples thought. It was crucial that they had no doubt about His identity. Peter's recognition of Jesus as "the Christ, the Son of the Living God" was much more than just a parroted response. He was not making a guess, saying what he thought would please Jesus, or going along with public opinion. His answer was the direct result of the Father's work in his heart. That's what Jesus meant when He said to Peter, "Flesh and blood did not reveal this to you, but My Father who is in heaven."

Countless people throughout the world consider themselves Christians because their parents are Christians, or because they have gone to church all their lives, or, like Dennis, because someone pressured them into praying the sinner's prayer. We should not be surprised then when we observe the following tendencies in these individuals: inability to grasp spiritual truth when it is proclaimed; failure to live victoriously over sin; constant struggling to feel excited about the Lord; and a lack of effective service in the church.

These people may enjoy the fellowship, the music and even the pastor's message. Often they will blend in well with the other believers and know how to say "praise the Lord" and "hallelujah" at the proper times. They can honestly say that they believe in God, and yet, they lack a true heart awareness of the reality of Christ. Jesus diagnosed their problem in Matthew 15:8 by saying: "This people honors Me with their lips, but their heart is far away from me." Verbal acknowledgment of the Lord is not enough. We must know Him personally.

It is no wonder that so many turn away from the Christian faith when the foundation of their faith is so flimsy. It is built upon the unstable ground of "head knowledge" alone, rather than on a God-given illumination of the Lord Jesus Christ and a genuine commitment of their hearts to Him. When afflictions, persecutions, or conflicting philosophies come against them, or when these people become distracted by the worries of the world or the value of earthly things, there is nothing to hold up their faith and they will fall away (Matt. 13:1-23; I Tim. 4:1-6).

Faith in Jesus alone is the only foundation strong enough to undergird us in the perilous times in which we live. First Corinthians 3:11 emphatically states: "For no man can lay a foundation other than the one which is laid, which is Jesus Christ." Even so, there are a variety of motivations for accepting Christ, and many different expectations as to what this involves. Some ask the Lord into their lives because they want His assistance with family problems. Others want Him to find them a job, or help them overcome a bad habit. A person's initial motivation for receiving Christ is very important, for it may lead to some deep feelings of disillusionment if his or her expectations do not come to fruition.

As an example, take the case of Ron, who was one of my best friends throughout my secondary school years. In my youthful zeal as a newborn Christian, I witnessed to him quite often, to such an extent that he became turned off by my pushiness.

"God loves you, Ron, and will meet all of your needs," I would tell him. "There isn't anything He can't do. If you'll just ask Him into your life, He'll help you with all your problems and never let you down!" I

5

was trying to make the gospel as appealing to him as possible so he would have little difficulty in receiving it. Nonetheless, he remained unwilling to make a commitment to the Lord.

Then one day Ron got kicked off the high school basketball team for misconduct. This was a real low point in his life because he loved basketball and felt embarrassed for having to leave the team. Being a faithful witness for Jesus (yet a very unwise one), I assured Ron that the Lord could put him back on the basketball team if he would pray with me to become a Christian. Having no alternatives and feeling it was worth a gamble, he finally asked Jesus to come into his life and put him back on the team. I was ecstatic to have a new convert, even though at times I had some doubts about his sincerity.

Amazingly, a few days later, Ron talked to the coach and was reinstated on the team. During the weeks that followed, he often gave thanks to God for the miracle that had happened. However, once his needs were met and he was able to get back into the same routine as before, he quickly lost his appreciation for what the Lord had done for him and began taking credit for it himself!

After a time, Ron encountered some other difficulties in his personal life which were not instantaneously corrected through prayer and God's intervention. These events led to the development of disillusionment in his attitude toward the Lord. After all, God was supposed to meet all of our needs at the snap of a finger, Ron had concluded (through listening to the Gospel According To Bob!). Eventually, he discovered that being a Christian wasn't always the bed of roses I had portrayed.

In fact, a conflict arose when Ron's understanding of God (as shaped by my one-sided comments) did not fit into the day-to-day reality that he was experiencing within himself. The discrepancy became so great between what he thought Christianity *should* be and what it actually was for him, that Ron began to question whether or not he wanted to be a Christian. In the weeks that followed, he unfortunately grew disenchanted with following Jesus and went back to his worldly way of life.

We must therefore be cautious about making lofty, speculative promises of how God will work to straighten out an unacceptable situation. To give such promises is misleading because it presents an erroneous picture of God to the earnest seeker. This approach sets the individual up for a catastrophic decline in his Christian faith because his experiences with Christ may not coincide with the distorted ideas he was given. Our Lord will not confine Himself to work according to our limited and often selfish anticipations. As God, He reserves the right to do whatever He pleases! (Isa. 46:9, 10)

Light Shall Shine Out Of Darkness

The Word of God tells us that some people will not be able to receive the message of Christ because of the way they approach Him. Jesus says the following in Matthew 11:25-27:

> I praise Thee, O Father, Lord of heaven and earth, that Thou didst hide these things from the wise and intelligent and didst reveal them to babes.
> Yes, Father, for thus it was well-pleasing in Thy sight.
> All things have been handed over to Me by My Father; and no one knows the Son, except the Father; nor does anyone know the Father, except the Son, and anyone to whom the Son wills to reveal Him.

Evaluating the teachings of the Scriptures solely on an intellectual basis will blindfold us to the truth. God's way of dealing with us is much different. Those who come to Christ in childlike dependence and teachability are the ones who will discover His reality in their lives.

The Apostle Paul was such a "child," for in the first chapter of Galatians he establishes the fact that he did not receive the gospel from a secondhand source. No one had brainwashed him into believing Christ's message! Instead, he had received his understanding of the Christian life directly from God Himself. The Father had, in Paul's words, "revealed His Son in me," and this realization profoundly changed his life. The Apostle states:

> For I would have you know, brethren, that the gospel which was preached by me is not according to man.

> For I neither received it from man, nor was I taught it,
> but I received it through a revelation of Jesus Christ (Gal.
> 1:11, 12).

The word "revelation" in this passage describes *God's initiative to disclose Himself* to Paul. The Apostle had received something from God that no man could take away. No one could talk him out of it. Persecution and unjust suffering were not enough to stamp it out. The truth of Christ had come alive in his heart — he had found the ultimate treasure of life!

Until God shines His light within us, we cannot fully understand or receive the blessings of knowing Jesus Christ. In Second Corinthians 4:6, Paul tells us: "For God, who said, 'Light shall shine out of darkness,' is the One who has shone in our hearts to give the light of the knowledge of the glory of God in the face of Christ." Paul is rejoicing here that although our minds were once closed as unbelievers, now the truth of God's Word has been made real to us and we will never be the same.

There is something vital, irreplaceable, and undefinable about having a sincere heart for God that has been warmed and won by personally beholding Him. We can witness to people about Jesus and get them to pray the sinner's prayer. We may even get them involved in an intense discipleship program, send them away to Bible school, or coerce them into a daily devotional routine, but one thing is for sure: there is no substitute for authentic devotion. This devotion is the work of the Holy Spirit in our hearts, for He inwardly motivates and infuses us with a genuine zeal for the Lord. We might expect that anyone who calls himself (or herself) a Christian would hunger and thirst for God. But this is obviously not true. Look at Dennis and Ron. Look at me.

Once our foundation has been made secure in Christ, we will evidence a durability and faithfulness in our Christian walk. No one will have to force us to become involved with a body of believers. And no one will have to pressure us to read the Bible and pray. Christian leaders won't have to make us feel guilty before we will witness. Instead, our joyous enthusiasm for God will be impossible to contain. Others will see that we have "been with Jesus," for we will radiate the glory of God by the smiles on our faces and the glow of our countenances (Acts 4:13). Having truly encountered the Risen Lord, we will be deeply convinced that He and He alone is worthy of our total devotion and praise.

Mental Assent or Genuine Conversion?

How can we be sure that our conversion experience is more than just mental assent to certain gospel truths? The following information will be of help:

1. *A genuine conversion involves turning to God with our whole heart and allowing His Spirit to change us.*

In Second Corinthians 3:14,15, Paul is contrasting the Old Covenant of the Law with the New Covenant initiated by Christ. He concludes (vss. 16-18) that, whereas the hearts and minds of the unbelieving world are hardened to the message of Jesus, those who come to Him will experience a significant transformation:

> ...but whenever a man turns to the Lord, the veil is taken away.
>
> Now the Lord is the Spirit; and where the Spirit of the Lord is, there is liberty.
>
> But we all, with unveiled face beholding as in a mirror the glory of the Lord, are being transformed into the same image from glory to glory, just as from the Lord, the Spirit.

Paul makes three important points here. First, when we turn to the Lord with sincerity of heart, He is faithful to remove any obstacles that keep us from seeing Him clearly. In this context, Paul was referring particularly to the number-one barrier of the Jews of his day — reliance on the Law as a means of justification before God (Rom. 3:20-31, 9:30-33). This tendency to make salvation depend upon our good works is a stumbling block to many of us today as well. There are also other barriers, such as pride, sinful habits, destructive thoughts, and the like, that hinder our relationship with God. The good news, though, is that *any* and *all* obstructions can be removed when a person turns his or her heart to the Lord!

9

Second, under the provisions of the New Covenant, we have perfect freedom to approach God without fear of condemnation or rejection (Rom. 8:1, 2). Nothing should deter us from coming close to Him, for as Paul reiterates in Ephesians 2:18, we have free "access in one Spirit to the Father."

Third, we are told to fix our gaze continually upon our glorious Lord Jesus Christ, because as we do, we will progressively be changed into His image. As we keep Christ at the center of our thoughts and actions, beholding Him in His fulness and majesty, we cannot help but be overwhelmed by His love and transformed by His awesome power.

2. *A genuine conversion occurs when the reality of the living Christ is birthed within us.*

Remember Dennis, whose involvement with Christianity was a dismal struggle until he truly met the Lord? Remember Ron, who appeared to receive Christ just to get help with his immediate problem? And there was my experience at the Ohio State Fair where I mumbled a sinner's prayer that did nothing for my life. Perhaps you have attended a church where the pastor or Sunday school teacher said all the right things, but with seemingly no effect. Or else you have failed to see significant growth in your life through reading the Bible or other Christian literature. The fact is that nothing can replace the life-changing impact of really knowing Christ personally.

The Holy Spirit speaks to us (through the Word, prayer, other Christians, and circumstances) in ways that will really make a difference. He never wastes words or time. The Spirit is no dispenser of theory — He knows exactly what we need to learn and He knows exactly how to teach it to us. When the Lord Himself reveals something to us, we are held captive to its message and our conscience is pricked until we respond to it. An open heart is all He needs.

3. *A genuine conversion has enduring value.*

We can see in the life of Paul that a victorious Christian walk requires more than just one encounter with Jesus. We must have an ongoing relationship with Him! The only reason Paul could endure such intense suffering for the sake of the gospel was that he kept his eyes on Christ and remained in intimate contact with Him. Consequently, no matter what difficulties came his way, he was able to stand firm, his faith unwavering (II Cor. 4:7-18). In Philippians 3:8, he makes the incredible claim: "I count all things to be loss in view of the surpassing value of knowing Christ Jesus my Lord, for whom I have suffered the loss of all things, and count them but rubbish in order that I may gain Christ."

Without solid roots in Him, we will not have the grace we need to stand strong in the midst of adversities. Any difficulty, regardless of its severity, could potentially overwhelm us. This need not happen. By growing in our understanding of God's Word, and allowing the Holy Spirit to illuminate the sufficiency of our Lord Jesus, there is no situation we cannot face with full confidence and complete triumph. Christ is the answer to every need we have. Whether we need love, or patience, or joy, or strength, or financial provision, or wisdom, there is no reason to become anxious or despairing — we have Christ and He is our source.

Reviewing Your Spiritual History

Have you failed to maintain a love relationship with Jesus because your conversion experience was based upon mental agreement to Christian principles rather than authentic devotion to Christ?

Or have you left your first love because your initial commitment to Him became weakened, sidetracked, and largely undeveloped from that point on?

If you are concerned that you have a head knowledge of the Lord but not a God-given illumination of His love to your heart, it isn't too late to do something about it. Why not pause right now and review your spiritual history? Are you certain there was a definite time in your life (or time period, if you don't know the exact date) when you committed yourself to Christ?

God wants to manifest Himself to you and give you the assurance of your salvation (Jn. 1:12; I Jn. 5:11, 12). This is more than just going to church because you were raised that way, or because some friends of yours thought it was a good idea. Rather, it is embracing the living Christ in such a way that it changes the self-centered direction in which you have walked. He is waiting for you to open the door of your life in an earnest desire to follow Him (Rev. 3:20).

11

If you aren't sure that Christ is in control in your life, take some time now and, in your own words, ask Him to forgive you of your sins and give you a brand-new start. Jesus not only promises us abundant life here on earth, He also provides an assurance of spending eternity with Him in heaven.

You may have had an initial encounter with the Lord, but have not maintained a vital, growing relationship with Him. Why not ask God to reverse this negative trend?

In the remainder of this book, we will discuss the major causes of spiritual degeneration in our Christian lives, along with some specific solutions found in God's Word.

2

DISTORTED CONCEPTS

When Michelle came into my office for counseling, she looked much older than her twenty years. Although she had received Christ into her life several years earlier, she still struggled with depression, self-hatred and thoughts of suicide. Michelle claimed there were barriers separating her from the Lord and she was unable to get close to Him. Everything she tried to do to make her situation better only made it worse. Michelle read her Bible more, prayed more, asked other Christians for advice and followed their instructions faithfully. Nothing helped — God seemed far away.

As I explored Michelle's background, I learned that her father, the pastor of a well-respected denominational church, "never had any time for her." He criticized Michelle constantly and expected her to act like a mature adult even when she was a small child. After all, "the preacher's daughter had to set a good example." All his pressure on Michelle to lead an exemplary life convinced her that she could never live up to his expectations. Since nothing she did was good enough to please him, she eventually came to see her father as unloving, demanding, and indifferent to her needs.

Michelle was handicapped by a problem that is very common. It is a well-established fact that our concept of God is often shaped by the way we perceive our parents, especially our fathers. Michelle looked at God, but saw her dad, which destroyed her motivation to draw near to Him. She was afraid that God, like her natural father, would reject her because she could never be good enough in His eyes.

Michelle's view of God was so distorted, it is no wonder she struggled in her relationship with Him! How can any of us eagerly pursue a God whom we perceive as unloving, demanding, and indifferent to our needs? Could we ever be convinced that such a God really loves us?

Our early, negative impressions of the Lord not only interfere with our desire to seek Him, but also with our ability to hear His voice. We tend to accept only that which fits into our preconceived notions of God and filter out the rest. If we see Him as a cruel taskmaster or a harsh judge, it will then be difficult to receive a message of His fatherly love for us. We will hear His loving words, but disregard them because they don't agree with our image of Him.

Those Christians who view God in an essentially positive way may also fall prey to erroneous thinking. We see this in the lives of a young couple named Rick and Marsha. They both came to the Lord as the result of dramatic conversion experiences, and were excited to know that God accepted them just the way they were. They gladly shared their testimonies with their families and other believers, and even accepted an invitation to speak at a nearby church.

Unfortunately, their concept of God did not take into account that He expects us to obey His Word. Rick and Marsha rationalized that God would not consider their living together outside of marriage as being a sin, since they were "so much in love." When a leader in their church told them they could not continue to call themselves Christians while living in immorality, they were deeply offended. As a result, they continued their living arrangement in secret, pretending to others that they were living apart.

This lie, which began with their refusal to take God's Word seriously, not only held back their individual growth, but obviously hindered them in relating to other believers. Since the specific word of correction from their church leader didn't fit into their concept of God, they rejected it.

Our Perspective or His?

We can see that our relationship with the Lord is strongly influenced by our notion of what He is like. Whenever we are faced with biblical teaching or revelation that contradicts our preconception of what is real and true, we must deal with the choice of embracing what God is speaking to us, or instead, tenaciously holding on to our distorted concepts. The result of hanging on to our own perspective is a handicapped relationship with God, for no relationship can grow properly in an atmosphere of unreality and deception.

Jesus encountered this kind of stubborn prejudice among the Pharisees. In contrast to Rick and Marsha's more permissive view of God, these religious leaders couldn't embrace Jesus' message since it didn't coincide with their rigid and narrow traditions. Jesus continually spoke of God as "the Father" and even went so far as to use the Aramaic word "Abba" to affectionately call God His "dad" (Mk. 14:36). The Pharisees placed their emphasis on God as their Creator and their Judge, a strict disciplinarian whose major interest was absolute and uncompromising obedience to the Law. Their God was not someone they could get very close to.

As a result, the Pharisees rejected Jesus' revelation of God as a compassionate Father, viewing it as arrogant, disrespectful and blasphemous. Regardless of Christ's incredible display of love and mercy through His many healings and miracles, the Pharisees were still unwilling to readjust their incorrect concept of God. What wonderful truths they rejected, all because they already had their minds made up! We should be careful lest we too fall into the same pattern of allowing our own narrow, predetermined ideas to keep us from receiving God-given insight concerning His nature and character.

This is essentially what happened to Michelle, the young lady mentioned at the beginning of this chapter. Her distorted view of God held her in bondage and made her afraid to receive the further truths our Lord wanted to reveal about Himself. She relied on her own ideas, memories and impressions to define God, and this erroneous perspective created a barrier in relating to Him. Although Michelle's initial experience with Jesus was very real to her, for all practical purposes, she was now shutting herself off from the fresh, ongoing revelation that was necessary for her spiritual vitality and overall growth in the Lord.

Whenever we open our Bible and find information that contradicts our previous thoughts of God, we are faced with a difficult decision. Should we embrace these new facts, even though they go against our picture of Him? Or, should we reject them because they don't fit in with what we've always believed? We may not be consciously aware that we are facing this decision.

Whatever the specific issue may be, it is important that we approach the Word of God prayerfully, asking the Lord to clear away our old, rigid concepts and make us receptive to new insights. When we turn our hearts and minds to God and give Him control over our understanding, we can expect to learn wonderful, life-giving truths about Him that we were never able to grasp before.

Have you left your first love because you have inaccurate ideas of who God is?

Self-Image and Our Walk with God

Another obstacle we encounter in receiving revelation from God is the way we perceive ourselves. There is an important connection between our self-image and how much truth we will be able to receive from Him. We all develop ideas about ourselves which are shaped by such factors as our family backgrounds, childhood experiences, the opinions of friends, and our failures and successes. These ideas form the basis of our self-concept, and our self-concept determines much of our view of reality. Let me explain.

Judy, a girl in her mid-twenties when I met her, viewed herself as being unattractive. For years she had felt extremely self-conscious because she was overweight. When she was growing up, Judy was often the object of cruel teasing from other children who called her "fat" and "ugly." She didn't understand why they would treat her so unkindly since she had never done anything to hurt them. Like many children in this kind of situation, she began to accept other people's negative evaluations and consequently developed an inferiority complex. Feeling hopeless about improving her situation, she resigned herself to the belief that she would always be an unlovable person.

Judy's ability to relate to other people was greatly hampered by her low self-esteem. In order to protect herself from further hurt, she frequently criticized her appearance and personality to keep others from doing it first. Her sense of humor became a means of deflecting hurt and she often joked about herself in a derogatory way. Judy eventually became unable to accept genuine compliments from other people, since such positive remarks contradicted her deeply-entrenched negative self-concept. By choosing to hold on to her predetermined view of herself, she rejected all attempts by others to point out her good qualities.

Thus, Judy's self-image became her gauge of reality, and a basis for making value judgments either to accept or reject the comments of other people. Positive comments were filtered out because she "knew" they were untrue; negative comments were accepted because she agreed with them.

Can you imagine the barriers Judy erected between herself and other people? Can you imagine the barriers that kept her from realizing the love of God?

Our self-concept often becomes a wall between us and God. Although He always desires to give us loving support, we too often screen out His positive input by demanding that it conform to our view of ourselves. If we are convinced we are unworthy of love, then we will not believe the Bible when it tells us that God loves us. If we judge ourselves unworthy of being forgiven, we will not agree with the Word when it tells us we are forgiven.

Have you left your first love because your poor self-image has built a wall around your heart, keeping Him away?

Tearing Down the Barricades

It is not enough to simply advise a person like Michelle to "lay aside her concept of God," or to tell Judy she must "forget her poor self-image." Such distortions have roots that run far deeper in our hearts and minds than we can ever comprehend. Although we often feel powerless to overcome these ingrained misconceptions, there is One who is more than qualified to help.

God.

God has the power to reach to the roots of a destructive concept and change it. God can undo the damage done by Michelle's earthly father by replacing her inaccurate concept of God with a true revelation of Himself. God can heal Judy's wounded heart and cause her to see herself in a brand-new way that is healthy and liberating.

Many of our own schemes and strategies for personal reform are based upon a limited knowledge of ourselves, others, and life in general, whereas God's wisdom transcends all finite understanding. He is all-knowing and loves us enough to be "intimately acquainted" with all our ways (Ps. 139:1-6). In fact, Jesus assures us of the personal love of God in Luke 12:6, 7, by saying:

> Are not five sparrows sold for two cents? And yet not one of them is forgotten before God.
> Indeed, the very hairs of your head are all numbered. Do not fear; you are of more value than many sparrows.

And in verse 32 of the same chapter, He adds:

> Do not be afraid, little flock, for your Father has chosen gladly to give you the kingdom.

Knowing the immense concern of God for your well-being, you can always approach Him with confidence. Jesus is talking to *you* when He says, "Do not fear." He is talking to *you* when He says, "Do not be afraid, little flock." Why would you recoil from One whose love is unfailing? Instead, let the revelation of God (which comes to us in Christ) break through the walls of your heart and renew your mind and spirit. Your willingness to be changed is all He needs to begin a glorious work that will tear down the barricades that separate you from His presence and filter out the sound of His voice.

Second Corinthians 10:5 says:

> We are destroying speculations and every lofty thing raised up against the knowledge of God, and we are taking every thought captive to the obedience of Christ.

This is good news! It promises us that every thought or opinion we may have that disagrees with God's Word can be destroyed. We do not have to live our entire lives in bondage to the kind of emotional damage Michelle and Judy suffered. *There is a way out!*

If we allow God to have control of our minds, emotions, and memories, He will then be able to change these aspects of our being so that they line up with His Word. He will open our eyes to see and experience the life-giving truth that He is the ultimate Father — compassionate, forgiving, and completely just.

A Distorted Notion of Christian Maturity

Jeff had been led to the Lord through the witnessing of some friends who were members of a Spirit-filled church. He had never felt so loved and accepted as he did on that day when he asked Christ into his heart. His Christian life seemed to be off to a great start.

However, Jeff's friends came from a church that placed strong emphasis on worship and the preaching of the Word. This may have been a good place for Jeff to grow in the Lord if he hadn't become so distracted by the people around him. The services were very different from those he was accustomed to, and although he was impressed with the enthusiasm of the people, he was uncomfortable with their expressions of praise. They punctuated the pastor's sermons with frequent amens. They clapped and raised their hands while singing and praying "oh, so loudly" during times of corporate prayer — and other aspects of their more vigorous approach to worship were new to him.

"This must be what I have to do to be spiritual," Jeff thought. "These people are all so far along in their walk with Christ! If I don't act like they do, God won't be too happy with me!"

Jeff began to blend into the church environment around him and to imitate the behavior of the other people. Along the way, he picked up some rather fuzzy ideas about what a "spiritual" person had to do to please God.

The other believers at church were soon impressed with the apparent progress Jeff was making. He attended as many meetings as anyone else; he quoted Bible verses just like everyone else; he was a faithful witness for Christ; and he had become very "good" at worship. Few people even suspected that inwardly Jeff was empty and unfulfilled in his Christian experience.

19

Jeff knew he wasn't contented. He sometimes wondered if this could really be the abundant life that Jesus had promised in John 10:10. But such thoughts made him feel guilty because he *knew* that dedicated Christians shouldn't even ask those kinds of questions. He tried to cover up his feelings because he had been taught that it wasn't very spiritual to reveal your weaknesses. Believing he wasn't measuring up to what God wanted from him, Jeff tried to work harder to live the perfect Christian life. He thought, "If only I would read the Bible a little more, evangelize more, and go to church more, surely I'd feel satisfied with my walk with the Lord."

Jeff's story is a sad one. Although his conversion experience was genuine, he wound up ridden with guilt and struggling to live what he considered to be a righteous life. Instead of seeking the Lord and growing naturally as a Christian, he became an actor, doing and saying all the right things outwardly, while inwardly feeling an increasing estrangement from God. By setting up his own rules and precepts (based on observing the people around him, and trying to follow them instead of the Lord), he encountered nothing but discouragement and confusion.

Have you left your first love because you didn't understand what He really wanted from you?

True Spirituality

We must be very careful to keep a proper perspective of what it means to be a "spiritual person" or else risk becoming sidetracked, like Jeff, and overwhelmed by frustration and guilt. Let's take a look at true spirituality. First, let me tell you what it is *not*.

It is not copying.

I was led to the Lord through the preaching of Billy Graham and have always admired him deeply. In fact, I wanted to be like him. I used to stand in front of the mirror and pretend I *was* Billy Graham, speaking to a multitude of people about the Lord.

After a time, God showed me that admiring Mr. Graham could be compared to admiring a fruitful tree. The fruit is easy to see, but the roots are hidden. There can be no fruit without solid roots underneath the tree. I was hoping my life would bear much fruit that would be readily visible to everyone. However, I had to learn that the real work of producing fruit takes place in the root system and goes unnoticed.

Our brothers and sisters in Christ may praise us for our outward display of Christianity and our conformity to their expectations and advice, but God is the One who searches our hearts. Appearances do not deceive Him, nor do they impress Him. This is good news. It assures us that true spirituality is a matter of our *relationship with God*, not of our performance.

We cannot expect our Lord Jesus to be pleased if we act like parrots. Our hollow repetitions of the right words and actions of others will never draw us closer to Him, and, in fact, will eventually push us farther away. This type of acting is essentially lying, for when we act, we are imitating behaviors and speaking words that do not come from our own hearts. Deceit can be carried on only so long before the frustration and futility of the performance wears us down.

So what *is* true spirituality?

It is being like Jesus.

And that happens only when we know Him.

We must look to Jesus, the author and perfecter of our faith (Heb. 12:2), as the standard of what God intends for us to be. If Christ is the center of our lives and we are yielded to His Spirit, then the expression of our faith will be pleasing to Him, regardless of whether we take on all the mannerisms of other Christians around us.

It is our personal relationship with Jesus Christ, then, that determines our spirituality, for we can only love Him if we know Him. And we can only know the Lord if we open our hearts to Him and seek Him in His Word, allowing Him to reveal Himself as He truly is.

Fine-Tuning Our Christian Faith

We have seen how our relationship with God can be seriously hindered by holding on to wrong ideas about Him. Like Michelle, we can miss the joy of knowing God as our Father because of distorted concepts we derived from negative experiences with parental authority. Like Judy, we can allow an overriding notion of our own worthlessness to filter out the words of love and encouragement God

21

would speak to us. Like Jeff, we can miss out on growing closer to the Lord because of erroneous ideas concerning true spirituality.

There is still another false concept that can interfere with our walk with God: making spiritual truths more complicated and exacting than they were meant to be.

Recently I attended a church leadership retreat. One man stood up and proclaimed, "I believe God is speaking to us that the only way we, as elders in the body of Christ, can effectively lead the people is by joining together on a regular basis for corporate prayer and fasting." The responses I observed to that exhortation have left a lasting impression on me. One by one, the other men at the retreat began to speak cautionary words to "balance out" what the first brother had said.

"That's true, we do need prayer, but we must be careful not to put ourselves under law when we pray. Prayer should be something we do because we want to — not because we have to."

"We must be aware that God is not interested in the quantity of our prayer, but the quality of our communion with Him."

"As we pray, let's not forget to pray in Jesus' name as the Scriptures teach us. In His name there is power to move mountains!"

"Yes, brother, but we need to spend time listening to God in prayer to know *which mountains* He wants removed in our lives. Sometimes we forget that when we pray, God wants to speak to us as well!"

For two hours, various men shared their concerns about how to pray effectively. As a result of hearing these additional, modifying statements, the original challenge for us to be committed to corporate prayer was obscured, then lost. In fact, the act of prayer itself had become greatly complicated by the twenty-plus suggestions we were to keep in mind in order to "pray the right way."

Rather than approach God in simplicity as those who longed to know Him, we now had a long check list of do's and don'ts to follow. A simple act of prayer had become complex, since we had to fulfill all the principles we had just heard in order to enter the presence of God with confidence. Consequently, our quest for "doing it right" distracted us from our main goal — doing it at all.

Simplicity and Purity

Second Corinthians 11:2, 3 states:

> For I am jealous for you with a godly jealousy; for I betrothed you to one husband, that to Christ I might present you as a pure virgin.

> But I am afraid, lest as the serpent deceived Eve by his craftiness, your minds should be led astray from the *simplicity and purity of devotion to Christ.*

There is a tremendous stress in our churches today on defining and redefining each aspect of our Christian lives. The Holy Spirit has been gracious to us in this generation by uncovering valuable insights from the Scriptures to help us see a greater glimpse of God's plan throughout the ages. Never before has there been such a wide selection of commentaries and original language aids to help us discover a more complete range of biblical truths.

We also have the privilege of drawing on the immense knowledge of all the precious men and women of God who lived throughout past centuries of church history. We cannot dispute that this accumulation of wisdom is helpful, yet we must be on guard that we do not become so caught up in our intellectualism that we lose the simplicity and purity of our devotion to Christ.

It is not uncommon to hear teachings or read booklets with the following titles:

"Fifteen Methods to Study the Bible"
"Thirty Ways to Lead a Person to Christ"
"Twenty-five Points to Remember When You Find
    Yourself in Sin"

Enumerating the various points of a given issue in an organized way is usually a helpful teaching device. It is a real blessing to see ministers of God's Word so concerned with clarity and balance in their teachings. However, in the maze of cautionary principles and explanatory words that we bring into a situation, we can sometimes lose sight of the essence of what God is trying to convey to us. We often tone down the specific word of conviction that God is speaking by confusing it with the many words we have added to balance it out.

We might compare this tendency to the Jewish scribes in Jesus' day. They strove to define from the Scriptures such statements as:

23

"Remember the sabbath day, to keep it holy" (Ex. 20:8), and in so doing, added scores of man-made regulations to what the Word actually said. Since they were uncomfortable when the commands of the Scriptures were not spelled out in detail, they developed their own set of clarifying precepts which went far beyond God's original intention.

In fact, the religious leaders of Judaism developed such a complex system of orthodox practice that they ignored some of the more important principles that God had established in the Law. Jesus rebuked them by saying:

> Woe to you, scribes and Pharisees, hypocrites! For you tithe mint and dill and cummin, and have neglected the weightier provisions of the law: justice and mercy and faithfulness; but these are the things you should have done without neglecting the others (Matt. 23:23).

How easy it is to lose our enthusiasm for the Lord if we feel we cannot take a step in our Christian lives without running into a number of complicated commands that must be precisely fulfilled. We may begin to believe it is impossible to please God in such devotional experiences as prayer and Bible study unless we perform twenty different rules to perfection. Sidetracked by a passion for exactness, we can lose the simplicity and the joy we once had in Christ. It is no wonder it is so difficult to enjoy a faith that has been analyzed to death! How can we approach God joyfully when we're shuffling our notes, trying to sort out what we have to say, what we need to remember, and how we're supposed to do it?

Have you left your first love because you have lost sight of Him somewhere in the man-made rules, pointers, and how-to's?

God wants to reveal Himself clearly, breaking through all our distorted concepts. God wants to reveal Himself compassionately, bringing His message of love and forgiveness through the barrier of our low self-images. God wants to reveal Himself and guide our growth at our needed pace, cutting through our false ideas of what spirituality is. God wants to reveal Himself in simplicity and purity, tuning out the distractions, and fine-tuning our faith to the sound of His voice. Our willingness is all He needs!

3

GUARDING YOUR HEART
(FROM THE ONE WHO LOVES YOU MOST)

In my years as a pastor, I've heard endless excuses as to why Christians aren't growing in the Lord. I remember a friend named Tom, who claimed, "I'd like to get closer to the Lord, but my job demands a lot from me and doesn't leave me with much time." Then there was Beth who told me, "I want to grow in my Christian walk, but I can't get the support I need from the church. Nobody has been reaching out to me!" Another believer named Roger usually responded to my queries about his walk with the Lord by shrugging and saying, "I just can't seem to get a handle on God's will for my life. He's sure keeping it a secret from me!" And there was Gigi, who always smiled broadly and said, "Everything's fine — just fine. I've got all I need."

At first glance, it may seem that these four Christians had widely varying responses, but in truth they all said the same thing. In essence, each one said, "I'm not growing in the Lord because I'm hiding from Him." Each of them employed a different "defense mechanism" which, in effect, constituted a carefully constructed wall around his or her heart to keep God from getting too close.

Defense mechanisms are patterns of behavior and response that are used to protect ourselves from other people. Oddly enough, we also use these same devices to protect ourselves from God.

Now, why would any Christian want to protect himself from God? Because God is the greatest possible threat to our lifestyles. He is interested in changing hearts, changing habits, and indeed, changing lives. And we can't hide ourselves from the eyes of an all-knowing God. As Hebrews 4:13 says:

> And there is no creature hidden from His sight, but all things are open and laid bare to the eyes of Him with whom we have to do.

Rather than open ourselves up to the change process that God brings into our lives (to make us more like Christ), we often erect barriers. Or, we scramble to protect ourselves, seeking to avoid any pain that might be involved in conforming to God's will. When our overall orientation is to "play it safe," our relationship with Him will inevitably suffer.

Four Ways We Protect Ourselves

One of the most common methods we use to defend our actions is **rationalization**. This approach is employed when we give explanations and excuses for our behavior that are meant to make our actions look better to ourselves and others. We even do this with our sin, working hard to redefine it in order to make it more acceptable. Like Tom, we find "good" reasons to explain our predicament, so good we even expect them to make an impression on God!

Have you ever heard statements like these?

> "I know I was speeding, officer, but I was late for work."
> "I always overeat when I'm nervous, and my boss has been driving me crazy."
> "I know God understands how I feel, so He won't mind if I miss church for a few weeks."
> "I know adultery is supposed to be wrong, but my wife doesn't love me and Lois really does."

By hiding behind these kinds of rationalizations, we hope to make our wrongdoing easier for ourselves and others (including God) to understand and accept. The excuses we give are an appeal for acceptance — a plea that others will understand what kind of helpless

26

condition we are in that keeps us from performing in the ways we should.

Blame shifting is another protective mechanism that shields our hearts from unwanted truth. This type of response occurs when we refuse to acknowledge our own guilt in a given matter and try to pin the blame either on circumstances or other people. The classic example of this occurs in Genesis 3, when Adam, confronted by God after his disobedience, explained that the woman the Lord had given him had caused him to sin. He not only tried to shift the blame to Eve, but also to God Himself for making her in the first place.

Perhaps you have attempted to absolve yourself from certain responsibilities by finding fault with others. Like Beth, you may have found a ready scapegoat for your problems in the failure of your church to support you in the way you had expected. Or, you may have sought out another set of shoulders to carry the blame for you when you failed.

Do any of these comments sound familiar?

> "I wouldn't miss church if my husband was more committed."
> "I'd love to go out witnessing, but my mother would be so embarrassed!"
> "I'd be a better Christian if I could grow at my own pace, but people demand too much of me. I need more time."

A third protective mechanism that is often used is a **confusion response**. This is a handy device we use when we claim we're so uncertain about what God wants from us that we are unable to change our behavior. People who hide behind this approach feel that if they can convince you they are totally confused about the problem they are dealing with, then they are free from all responsibility to overcome it. By playing upon their supposed helplessness, they try to gain the sympathy of others.

> "My mind is spinning around — I just don't know what God wants me to do!"

27

"Whenever I think about my problem, I get so depressed and frustrated! There just doesn't seem to be a way out for me."

"I'd like to forgive my parents, but I'm not sure how to go about it."

If these people can successfully convince you that they are terribly confused, they feel safe in believing that you have no right to pressure them to change. After all, how can they be held accountable for what they don't understand?

This same principle also applies to our relationship with God. It is truly amazing how often we justify disobedience to the specific commands of the Scriptures by claiming not to understand them.

"I can't see why God wouldn't allow John and me to live together before we marry. We really love each other."

"If only I understood what Jesus meant by loving your enemy, then I could get along with Agnes."

Another hindrance to our growth in the Lord is **self-reliance**. Someone once said, "You are where you are in your relationship with God because *that's where you want to be.*" Did you know that we can decide just how much we will receive from the Lord? If we are satisfied with our lives as they are, we won't be open to the additional things God might want to teach us or do for us. Our self-reliance closes the door in His face. It acts as a selective filter to spiritual truth, keeping out that which demands too much change or self-sacrifice. We hear and accept all the Scriptures that bless us and fit into our current lifestyle, and tune out the ones that challenge us to change.

Many Christians who say they are "saved," or that they "love the Lord" have little sensitivity to hearing and obeying His voice. They are content to know that they are going to heaven someday and have escaped the wrath of God. Their church involvement has become little more than just weekly church attendance, enjoyment of the music, and half their attention when the pastor speaks. Since these church-goers are not engaging in gross outward sins, they often feel their lives must therefore be pleasing to God. Content and complacent, they "stand still in their walk" and assure their companions, as Gigi did, that everything is just fine. It is, to them. It isn't, to God.

Self-reliant attitudes also show up in another form. When God uses us in a special way, we often take note of the exact behaviors that were happening at the time His blessings came. We are then tempted to emulate (by our own efforts) the same actions and procedures we were doing when God's Spirit was working through us. Since our behavior under these circumstances may *look* exactly the same as it did before, we could easily assume, in a prideful way, that *our own effort* produced a genuine fruit of the Spirit (Gal. 5:22, 23).

However, real fruit is the product of His Spirit working in us — and not just a set of behaviors we have learned. Our own efforts to produce or imitate the Holy Spirit's fruit will always be shallow and limited. By losing sight of our own weaknesses and the need for His grace, we will hinder what God will be able to accomplish in our lives. For we will only receive from Him what we're convinced we need!

Consequently, it is important to distinguish between our *true* needs and *perceived* needs that are just personal preferences. When we define something as a need, there's a sense of urgency we attach to fulfilling it. A genuine frustration occurs when these supposed needs remain unsatisfied.

As we bring each area of our lives before the Lord in a sincere desire to walk in His truth, we might find that what we felt to be a necessity was merely a selfish desire. In fact, we may even discover later, to our surprise, that the fulfillment of our perceived need would have led to shipwreck in our Christian lives. We can rest assured that our God, a God of love, knows our needs better than we do and we can trust Him to act in our best interests. His Word clearly promises: "And my God shall supply all your needs [not greeds!] according to His riches in glory in Christ Jesus" (Phil. 4:19).

Have you left your first love because you have built protective barriers around your heart that are keeping Him out?

My Sheep Hear My Voice

My brother Jim (who is three years older) and I both received Christ while we were in high school. We each had a desire to tell others about Jesus, but Jim was clearly the bolder one. He had no inhibitions at all about going into the most precarious situations and proclaiming the gospel. In fact, he would evangelize anywhere he could get an audience. He shared the Lord in restaurants, children's homes, nursing homes, schools, public parks — anywhere.

Jim always wanted me to go with him whenever he went out witnessing. Since I was easily intimidated and didn't want to risk losing the respect of others, I was hesitant to go. Yet, he was relentless in prodding me along.

"Let's pray about where we should go," Jim would say, and then he would rattle off a list of possible places. "I'm sure the Lord will tell us!"

It was this last statement that would bother me the most, since I never seemed to be able to hear God speak to me when I prayed. To be honest, when Jim began challenging me to listen to God's voice, I wasn't even sure what he was talking about. So we would pray and wait upon the Lord, and after a few minutes, he would ask me, "Well, Bob, what is God saying to you?" I rarely had any clearcut answers for him. This was discouraging to me, since Jim seemed so much more confident in knowing how the Lord was directing him.

Difficult as it was, I found myself intrigued with learning to receive God's guidance. Jesus' statements in John 10:14, 27 made me aware of my shortcomings:

> I am the good shepherd; and I know My own, and My own know Me....
> My sheep hear My voice, and I know them, and they follow Me....

Jesus is telling us that He knows each believer in an intimate way, and that we can also know Him personally. Yet, the passage goes on to say that we cannot separate *knowing the Lord* from *hearing His voice* and receiving guidance from Him. You can imagine how I felt about that! I saw other Christians — my own brother among them — confidently seeking the Lord's will in very specific situations, and receiving it. But as for me, I knew very little at the time about hearing the Shepherd's voice.

Learning to Listen

I began to realize early in my walk with the Lord that He is looking

30

for functional Christians who are not merely satisfied with having the hope of eternal life for the *future*. He wants our lives to be useful to Him *right now!* He is looking for people who can detect the leading of the Holy Spirit and willingly respond.

How can we hear God's voice? The first step is to know His Word. Psalm 119:105 tells us:

> Thy word is a lamp to my feet, and a light to my path.

Before we can expect to receive fresh revelation and instruction from God, we must first have a firm grasp on what He has already said. Second Timothy 3:16, 17 clearly states:

> All Scripture is inspired by God [lit. "God-breathed"] and profitable for teaching, for reproof, for correction, for training in righteousness;
> that the man of God may be adequate, equipped for every good work.

As the truths of His Word are carefully applied to our lives, we will be secure in His wisdom and "equipped for every good work."

Think back to the section on confusion response. Each one of the questions asked by the mixed-up Christians are plainly addressed in God's Word. We don't have to live in a state of confusion, stymied by questions that God has already answered for us in the Bible. We won't ask God to tell us whether or not we should live together without being married — we'll know exactly how He feels about it. We won't expect Him to hit us with thunderbolts of conviction before we recognize our own sin of pride and hostility directed toward our parents. We won't wonder if it's all right to lie to our spouse — the Bible says it's wrong.

This, then, is the first step toward receiving guidance from God: learn the Word. When you know the Scriptures, you begin to know God. And God is faithful to make His Word come alive to those who are receptive to it. He will teach you things you never imagined, and give you a solid, unshakable set of standards that will clear away the confusion about how to handle your daily conflicts and relationships.

The second step is learning to hear God's voice when He speaks to you by His Spirit. Those who hear God are those who are listening. Look again at John 10:14, 27. Jesus says, "My own know Me. . . my sheep hear My voice, and I know them....." Rarely does God speak distinctly to an unbeliever. That sensitivity is for Christians who have learned to walk daily beside the Good Shepherd and yield their hearts to the leading of His Spirit.

If someone I have never met calls me on the telephone and begins speaking without mentioning his or her name in the conversation, I would be unable to identify the person. Yet, when my wife calls me, she doesn't have to introduce herself by saying, "Hi, Bob, this is your wife." I already know her voice. Over time, I have learned to recognize it.

This is the way it is in our relationship with God; becoming able to hear His voice is a learning process. It takes time to become familiar with the various ways He communicates. Some believers say that God speaks in a "still, small voice," while others describe their experiences as an inward impression, a spontaneous thought, or a picture that flashes across their mind. Regardless of how we verbalize it, the important thing is to grow in our awareness of how God speaks and in our capacity to detect the impressions He brings our way. Whether He speaks directly to our hearts (through His Word or His Spirit), or indirectly (through other people or specific circumstances), we must not harden our hearts.

But what about those who are barricaded behind defense mechanisms? Does God speak to them? He wants to. Hebrews 3:7,8 admonishes us:

Therefore, just as the Holy Spirit says,

Today if you hear His voice,
Do not harden your hearts....

We may find ourselves crying out for a new word from God and some amazing revelation of truth — but have we fully obeyed Him in the last thing He clearly called us to do? Perhaps we have rejected certain information we didn't want to receive, filtering it through our defenses until it had no effect on us. God cannot speak and be heard if He is trying to get through to a person who rationalizes inactivity and disobedience; or who shifts the blame for his or her own failings onto other people or circumstances; or who feigns a lack of understanding of God's will; or who is stubbornly contented with a Christian walk that doesn't go anywhere; or who has become hardened because of repeated unwillingness to receive scriptural truth.

The promise of God is clear — He will readily receive us into an intimate relationship with Him if we truly desire it. James 4:8 tells us: "Draw near to God and He will draw near to you." Through the precious Holy Spirit, He will speak to us and guide us into all truth. As John 16:13 states:

> But when He, the Spirit of truth, comes, He will guide
> you into all the truth; for He will not speak on His own
> initiative, but whatever He hears, He will speak; and He
> will disclose to you what is to come.

Let us examine ourselves prayerfully, asking God to show us those barriers we have erected around our hearts to keep His Word and will from penetrating and changing us. Let us also willingly put aside our excuses, our complaints, our confusions, our complacency, and our self-reliance, and seek Him afresh in His Word and in prayer, allowing Him to break down our defenses, knock down our barriers, and have unimpeded fellowship with us.

Have you left your first love because you have failed to hear His voice?

4

RESTORING YOUR SPIRITUAL YOUTHFULNESS

A short time ago there was a movie on television about a famous actress in the 1950's who, for a number of reasons, had a serious mental breakdown which resulted in her being hospitalized. Although it seemed that this beautiful and talented entertainer would have unending success, the strain of her new-found stardom, her broken marriage, sexual immorality, and unresolved bitterness toward her parents sent her life into a tailspin.

The best psychiatrists were of little help. She wound up in a deplorable mental institution, a shattered, confused human being. As her condition worsened, she completely withdrew from having meaningful relationships with other people around her. She also lost her motivation to take care of herself. Her hair began to fall out, her teeth started to rot, and she became as skinny as a rail because of her unwillingness to eat a well-balanced diet. Even though she was once heralded as an "exceptional communicator," her thought processes were now scattered and her words were largely nonsensical.

This woman was still relatively young, but for all practical purposes, she evidenced the wear and tear of old age. When she lost her hope and reason for living, the normal aging process rapidly accelerated.

In a similar way, there are a number of Christians who are relatively young in the Lord, but already evidence the characteristics of what can be called "spiritual old age." The resulting symptoms closely parallel the same conditions we often observe in those older people who have become set in their ways: unteachableness, loss of flexibility, a focus on past events, and an inward orientation to life.

Characteristics of Spiritual Old Age

1. *Unteachableness.* The longer a person lives, the more opportunities he or she will have to learn. And yet, the older we become, the more likely we are to assume we know all we need to know on a given subject. We then cut ourselves off from additional learning and refuse to accept the opinions, advice, or corrections of other people.

A lovely woman named Grace, who had taken care of the altar at her church for nearly forty years, became depressed over a personal failure in her life and decided to punish her sin by denying herself communion.

Even though her pastor and friends gently pointed out that this was not God's desire for her, she steadfastly refused to listen and shut herself off from the very thing Jesus gave us as a way of drawing close to Him. Her depression deepened and she eventually quit going to church, still convinced that she was doing the right thing.

In much the same way, the older we are in the Lord, the more stubborn and less teachable we often become. A new Christian might come up to us and say, "Wow! I just discovered God loves me and forgives all my sins!"

We might respond to such enthusiasm with a demeaning, "Of course He does. I've known that for years — it's a truth that all beginners need to learn." Assuming that we have gone beyond the elementary teachings of God's love and forgiveness, we conclude this new believer has nothing new to teach us. However, we are greatly mistaken — God can use anybody at any time for our instruction.

It is unfortunate when older Christians compare themselves to others and decide they have arrived at a sufficient level of spirituality. They may then develop judgmental attitudes towards other believers who are not as knowledgeable. When their "mature and seasoned" point of view is not accepted, they often become offended. These Christians tragically have forgotten how many years it took them to get where they are in the Lord and how many changes the Holy Spirit has made in their personalities.

2. *A loss of flexibility.* As we become older, we often prefer to have the events of our lives conform to a consistent routine. It isn't easy for us to adapt to rapid, dramatic changes. By structuring our lives in a predictable manner, we avoid the threat of uncertainty and maintain a sense of control.

I know of one elderly gentleman who lived by such a rigid clock that any interruption would ruin his entire day. Every morning he put on his plaid jacket and walked outside to the driveway to pick up his newspaper. His grandson's wife, who had come to visit him, beat him to it one morning, and the unaccustomed change in routine upset him so much he had to retreat to his room to regroup his emotions. What most of us would consider to be a small incident left him completely out of sorts the rest of the day.

In much the same way, when we lose our spiritual youthfulness, we are only comfortable with a Christianity that does not cause us to deal with the insecurity of unexpected changes. We begin to "require" God to act within the narrow confines of our human understanding and to fit into our expectations of what He will and will not do. It is easier to relate to a God who is predictable, who assures us that He will not rock the boat and demand overwhelming changes from us. But, in so doing, we become satisfied with a mere mechanical performance of our traditions, since these activities can take place with little or no dependence upon God. In contrast, those who are still youthful in the Lord are open to any work of the Holy Spirit, even if it involves major changes and the loss of their feelings of comfort and control.

3. *Focus on past events.* During the latter years of life, it is common to focus on memories of the past. Older people characteristically reminisce about the highlights of their lives, and how interesting these stories can be! Yet, preoccupation with the past can block out the enjoyment of the present.

There are many Christians who begin with a powerful revelation of God's love and grace, but do not continue to stay in touch with Him.

They try to live off the strength of their initial experience. George was such a man. One evening he attended a revival meeting with a friend and eagerly accepted the invitation to receive Jesus as his Lord and Savior. It was apparent to everyone that George had been deeply affected and gloriously converted by his encounter with the Lord.

Six months later, the pastor saw George in the back of the church (by now he was a regular attender) and invited him to give a testimony. George went forward enthusiastically and exclaimed, "Just six months ago, I knelt here at this altar and gave my life to Christ. It was a tremendous experience!"

At an evening service two years later, the pastor again pointed to George, and said: "We haven't heard from you in quite awhile. Please come forward and bring us up-to-date on what is happening in your walk with the Lord."

George went to the microphone and proclaimed, "Two years ago, right here at this altar, I gave my heart to Jesus and it was a real blessing — in fact, it was the best thing I ever did."

Ten years after his conversion, George was again invited to share what the Lord was doing in his life. This time he walked slowly to the microphone and responded, "Right here at this very altar, ten years ago now, I dedicated myself to Jesus. It was the greatest moment of my life."

What was wrong with George's Christian walk? Even though he once had a life-changing encounter with Christ, he failed to cultivate a fresh, daily relationship with Him. He relied on his past testimony, losing sight of the fact that God desired to do a continual work in his life. Fixed in a safe, but static, Christian experience, he stopped growing, changing, accepting challenges, and learning. His spiritual walk was leading him nowhere.

4. *An inward orientation.* Hal's dream had finally come true. After working for a local electric company for more than thirty years, he had just retired. From his perspective, he was set for the rest of his life — a good pension plan; excellent health; three children who were raised and on their own; few expenses; and so much more.

What a relief he felt! No longer did he have to face the pressure of going to work each day and providing for his family. All the former restraints were gone and he could do whatever he wished. It was time to enjoy himself. "I've lived for others all these years," he concluded. "It's time to start living for myself!"

Hal's story reminds us of another characteristic of spiritual old age — an inward orientation in life. He had once served others and focused on their welfare, but now he felt it was time to "look out for Number One." By tuning into himself and his own interests, Hal consequently tuned out the needs of others.

We might parallel the events of this story to what can happen in our spiritual lives. Having once had an outward focus that motivated us to extend ourselves to others in love, after a time we may selfishly turn inward. We feel that we already have more burdens than we can possibly handle and don't need anything else to deal with. As a result, we gravitate toward taking care of ourselves and miss opportunities to reach out for Christ to those around us.

Like Hal, we may even feel justified in our self-centered condition. We see ourselves as stretched to the limit, pushed beyond our energy level, and weary from coping with the pressures of life. To protect ourselves from overextension and burnout, we retreat. But how can we justify failing to devote any of our time to helping others find Christ? Have we lost our compassion and forgotten our calling as Christians to minister to the hurting people around us?

In Matthew 5:13-16, Jesus gives two metaphors — salt and light —to describe how we, as His followers, should influence the world:

> You are the salt of the earth; but if the salt has become tasteless, how will it be made salty again? It is good for nothing any more, except to be thrown out and trampled under foot by men.
>
> You are the light of the world. A city set on a hill cannot be hidden.
>
> Nor do men light a lamp, and put it under the peck-measure, but on the lampstand; and it gives light to all who are in the house.
>
> Let your light shine before men in such a way that they may see your good works, and glorify your Father who is in heaven.

Implicit in these two examples is the truth that the people of God are to remain distinctly different from the world while still making a positive impact on it.

In biblical days, salt was primarily used as a seasoning (giving an appetizing taste to food) and as a preservative (to arrest the decay of freshly-cut meat). Jesus is making a significant point in this message. If salt loses its saltiness, how can it fulfill its intended purposes? In much the same way, light, which is meant to drive away the darkness, remains useless as long as it is concealed. Thus, Christians are supposed to have a powerful effect on the world — as salt, to hinder the decay of our deteriorating society, and as light, to dispel the darkness of sin.

Jesus is warning us that it is possible to become ineffective in our witness to the world through losing our saltiness (our positive influence for righteousness), and by covering over the light of Christ so that the world cannot see. These two illustrations are vivid examples of spiritual regression in our lives. When this occurs, we cease to glorify our Heavenly Father and become useless in establishing His kingdom throughout the earth (Lk. 14:34, 35). What a tragedy to see God's people in this condition!

God began to deal with me in this area a few years ago when several people from our church went door-to-door in an inner-city neighborhood to witness for Christ. As the pastor of an evangelical church, I was spending nearly all of my time with other Christians. Convicted by the realization that it had been quite a while since I had a one-on-one conversation about Christ with a non-believer, I was determined to go.

Something significant happened to me as I took advantage of the opportunities to share my faith in the Lord. Through proclaiming His goodness to the people we met, I myself experienced an inward revival and a renewed vision for my Christian walk! I had a rekindled awareness of the love of Jesus as I spoke to others about that love.

We must admit that too few Christians have ever led another person to the Lord. Even those who have helped others to find Christ often concede that many of these "converts" are no longer walking with Him. In fact, whole congregations of believers have completely withdrawn themselves from the world and have grieved the Holy Spirit by losing their evangelistic fervor. We tend to avoid the challenge of witnessing to non-Christians by pursuing a course which is less threatening and demanding to our faith. But if our faith remains unchallenged, how can it grow?

Youth Renewed Like the Eagle

It is important to examine your life in light of these four characteristics of spiritual old age. If any or all of these qualities are currently a part of your Christian experience, you can receive encouragement from a well-known Old Testament passage:

> Though youths grow weary and tired,
> And vigorous young men stumble badly,
> Yet those who wait for the Lord
> Will gain new strength;
> They will mount up with wings like eagles,
> They will run and not get tired,
> They will walk and not become weary
> (Isa. 40:30, 31).

Isaiah is referring to the ability of eagles to glide with ease on the strength of an existing air current. While other birds seem to fly by flapping their wings and exerting a lot of their own energy, the eagle calmly perches on the edge of a cliff and waits for a gust of air before launching out. The blowing wind provides the impetus forward; the eagle patiently waits for it and begins its flight accordingly. By moving ahead on the strength of the air current, the eagle can soar at high altitudes seemingly without effort or restraint.

Perhaps you are a person whose life evidences spiritual old age. If so, God wants to restore your youthfulness! He will refresh you in His presence and renew you in His love. And He will teach you to soar like an eagle in the rushing, mighty wind of His Spirit (Acts 2). But you must learn to wait for the Lord, for "He gives strength to the weary, and to him who lacks might he increases power" (Isa. 40:29).

The phrase "those who wait for the Lord" (Isa. 40:31) can also be translated, "yet those who hope in the Lord will gain new strength." We cannot move ahead in the Christian life by wildly flapping our wings—we must learn to move ahead in the power of His Spirit. In other words, our hope for spiritual progress must be anchored in God alone.

Have you lost your hope today that God will renew the days of your youthful zeal and vitality? Do you feel that you have wasted a lot of time and have been a failure in the Lord's eyes? It's time to turn back to Him with your whole heart! He will renew your strength and rejuvenate you so that the following signs of *youthfulness* will appear in your Christian walk: teachableness, flexibility, ongoing growth, and compassion in reaching out to others. As the Psalmist so beautifully adds: He will satisfy ". . . your years with good things, so that your *youth is renewed like the eagle*" (Ps. 103:5).

5

BARRENNESS IN BUSYNESS

Gerald became a Christian when he was a freshman in college and he quickly gained a reputation as one who was zealous for God. He was the kind of person you never had to motivate in his devotional life, spending several hours each day reading the Bible and praying. In fact, it was difficult to get Gerald to do anything else! His schoolwork and the pursuit of a career hardly seemed important to him anymore. Somehow Gerald managed to get by the rigors of the academic scene, even though he spent very little time studying. He was consumed with his desire to witness for Christ and to strengthen other believers on campus.

After graduation, Gerald took a job with a large corporation, and a few months later he married a nice Christian girl. In the next five years, he and his wife were "fruitful and multiplied," adding three beautiful children to the family. Gerald usually spent from fifty to sixty hours a week at work and quickly climbed the corporate ladder. Even though he was often quite tired after a hard day at the office, he always managed to find time to spend with his family. He was determined not to forsake his God-given responsibility to love and nurture his wife and raise his children in a proper way. Sounds like the ideal Christian home, doesn't it? Not quite.

There was a critical ingredient missing in Gerald's life. Dealing with the daily pressures he encountered not only sapped his energy, but robbed him of time he needed with the Lord. Gone were the days when he could spend hour after hour engrossed in Bible study and prayer. Now it was a struggle for him just to include a few minutes a day alone with God in his busy schedule. Actually, there were days when Gerald ignored Him altogether.

"The Lord understands how swamped I am," he rationalized. "It's just not as easy as it used to be to find time with Him."

There was much truth in Gerald's perspective — it certainly wasn't as *easy* for him to set aside some quiet moments for God. This was a new phase of life and much had changed. The stress of handling work obligations and providing for his family was extremely taxing on him. As he shouldered more and more responsibilities, he perpetually struggled to use his time wisely. In fact, he felt that his whole existence was consumed with trying to successfully juggle his priorities. Should Gerald be rebuked for being complacent, or were the changes that happened in his spiritual life inevitable?

We all face the problem of losing sight of Jesus in the crowded events of the day. Jesus Himself spoke to this issue in Luke 17:26, 27, using both Noah and Lot from the Old Testament as examples:

> And just as it happened in the days of Noah, so it shall be also in the days of the Son of Man:
> they were *eating*, and they were *drinking*, they were *marrying*, they were being given in marriage, until the day that Noah entered the ark, and the flood came and destroyed them all.

After reading this passage, we may ask, "What is wrong with eating, drinking, and getting married? They are all a part of normal, everyday living!" Jesus speaks further:

> It was the same as happened in the days of Lot: they were *eating*, they were *drinking*, they were *buying*, they were *selling*, they were *planting*, they were *building*;
> but on the day that Lot went out from Sodom it rained fire and brimstone from heaven and destroyed them all.

It will be just the same on the day that the Son of Man is revealed (Lk. 17:28-30).

Obviously, Jesus is not condemning eating, drinking, buying, selling, planting, and building. If He was, we would all be in trouble! He was condemning our *excessive preoccupation* with these things, preoccupation that dulls us to the sound of His voice. When God spoke from heaven to warn the people of the impending flood, Noah was the only one on earth who could hear what He was saying. Everyone else was engaged in worldliness and sinful pursuits (Gen. 6:5-22). Likewise, when the Lord gave warning of the impending doom of Sodom and Gomorrah, Abraham, free from the treadmill of daily living, heard God speak and was able to intercede in prayer for Lot (Gen. 18:16-33). In contrast to both Abraham and Noah, we can become immersed in our routines and absorbed in the trials of life to the extent that we shut out what God wants to communicate to us.

We sometimes discover that as soon as we become comfortable in relating to God and trusting Him in the more predictable circumstances of the present, He then calls us to adjust to a different phase of life (a new job, a new town to live in, another child, the death of a loved one, or a broken relationship, among other things). The new events that enter our lives will generate fresh challenges, fluctuating emotions, and tough decisions. And as a result, our faith will be stretched and our real values will rise to the surface.

During these times of transition, we may assume that we are now strong enough in the Lord to slack off a little at this stage of our Christian experience. We rationalize that we can always make up for lost time later, and that we'll give ourselves to God more completely when things settle down. The problem is that things never seem to settle down — myriads of concerns cry out for our attention in each period of life.

Have you left your first love because you are preoccupied with worldly cares and concerns?

A Desire For Closeness

During my senior year in high school, I would often begin my mornings by praying, "Lord, I want You to be in complete control of my life today. Help me to keep my eyes on You and not get caught up in everything that is going on around me." And yet, practically every night before I went to bed, I would apologize to God for going hours and hours throughout the day without even thinking about Him. My mind seemed overloaded with thoughts of school, athletic pursuits, family activities, and social events. The Lord was crowded out.

Then I had a brainstorm! Why not wear two rubber bands on my fingers to remind me of God? If the rubber bands were tight enough, my attention would be arrested and, through the process of association, I would turn my thoughts to Him. When I implemented my plan, I found that it did help me somewhat — but how flustered I became when a couple of girls asked me why I was wearing the rubber bands! I explained nervously that one rubber band reminded me "I need the Lord at all times," and the other one stood for "He's always with me." I was glad for the opportunity to be a witness to them, but I was embarrassed by such a meager attempt to meet what I felt was a pressing need in my life.

Perhaps you are concerned that you aren't as close to the Lord as you should be. Are you trying to define "closeness" with God solely on the basis of the amount of time you now spend with Him, while overlooking some larger issues? God's most important concern is the condition of your heart. If your heart is fully His, you'll do all you can to set aside consistent, quality time for Him.

Stressful circumstances and demanding obligations will come and go during each transition of life, but we must learn to face them with God's help. It's vital for us to become aware of His priorities and to be firmly committed to carrying them out in the power of the Spirit. We can't afford to become complacent and waste valuable time that could be useful to our Christian growth with the expectation that easier days will come.

Satan loves for us to condemn ourselves when our present circumstances do not seem to match up favorably with our past performance. As we compare our former zeal to our current struggle, we may either succumb to discouragement (through seeing ourselves as failures), or else come up with endless excuses for our spiritual decline (blaming it on the tough road we must walk). Certainly God would have us place a high priority on our schoolwork, family, and careers, but even these things, which are good, should never over-shadow the Lord and His preeminence in our lives!

Seek First The Kingdom

In Matthew 6:31-33, Jesus addresses the issue of establishing right priorities:

> Do not be anxious then, saying "What shall we eat?" or "What shall we drink?" or "With what shall we clothe ourselves?"
>
> For all these things the Gentiles eagerly seek; for your heavenly Father knows that you need all these things.
>
> But seek first His kingdom and His righteousness; and all these things shall be added to you.

Here again, Jesus is not teaching against making legitimate preparations for eating, drinking, and being clothed. He is criticizing those who focus their attention on gaining material needs, while minimizing the more important spiritual issues of life. Instead, He wanted His followers to be free of anxiety, trusting the Father's willingness to meet their needs.

What does it mean to seek first the kingdom? Simply put, there are two elements of any kingdom; a king and some people over whom the king rules. Thus, the kingdom of God refers to the realm in which God rules. When we seek first the kingdom of God, we are submitting ourselves to Him and acknowledging His right to reign supreme in our lives. He desires to extend His dominion across the face of the earth so that every person willingly acknowledges Jesus Christ as Lord and Savior. Placing the kingdom of God first in our lives involves *yielding ourselves* to Him and *actively participating* in the advancement of the gospel to the unreached people of the world.

Someone once said, "If the kingdom of God is worth *anything*, it must be worth *everything* to us." Therefore, our values must be "kingdom values" and not the materialistic values of our society. Our time schedule should be reflective of our commitment to God and His kingdom. Our financial expenditures should include generous giving to advance Christian work around the world. How we spend our time, money, and energy clearly reveals what is really important to us.

Let's not kid ourselves anymore. Do our lifestyles presently reflect godly priorities, or are they virtually indistinguishable from the average non-believer? Oh, yes, much about Christians and those who are outside the faith is the same — we all must go to school, work, engage in family activities, eat, drink, buy, sell, etc. But we, as believers in Christ, live under a different set of values than those without the Lord. We have put the advancement of His work on the earth as our number-one priority, ahead of all else. All of our commitments are then evaluated in light of our supreme calling — to bow our knees to God and see others do the same.

It is not enough to mentally believe in Christ; or to feel good about what others are doing to see the nations won to Him; or to pray an occasional prayer for world evangelism. We must make it a priority to structure our lives around this one great quest of seeing God's rule and reign extended throughout the earth.

Some people have the special privilege of giving themselves to full-time Christian service and are supported financially by God's people for their endeavors. But the vast majority of believers must walk the same path as Gerald, working forty-plus hours a week and trying to manage family, educational, and recreational activities in the most productive way.

It is certainly not wrong to be busy, for busyness is a part of life. And yet, busyness should not be an excuse for spiritual complacency or wrong values. The problem is, when it's all said and done, where is the time and energy left over for God? Furthermore, if the Lord is only getting our left-over time, money, and energy, can we really say we are seeking first His kingdom? Shouldn't Jesus and His concerns be the dominant focus of our lives? Have we gotten caught up in our own little world? Are we living a self-indulgent life? Have we forgotten the mission God has called us to accomplish, a mission that is far from being done? (Matt. 28:18-20; Mk. 16:15).

48

Be Filled With The Spirit

In my search to keep Jesus as the constant focus of my life, the Lord showed me a better way than rubber bands! Better than rubber bands? Yes. He brought me to a deeper place of consecration and filled me in a glorious way with His Spirit! As I learned to abide in Him and look to Him to satisfy the longings of my heart, the Lord's presence was much more evident throughout each day.

We can try all kinds of strategies to get closer to God, but there is no replacement for having God Himself fill our lives to overflowing with His Spirit. Paul tells us in Ephesians 5:18-21:

> And do not get drunk with wine, for that is dissipation, *but be filled with the Spirit*, speaking to one another in psalms and hymns and spiritual songs, singing and making melody with your heart to the Lord;
> always giving thanks for all things in the name of our Lord Jesus Christ to God, even the Father;
> and be subject to one another in the fear of Christ.

A pastor in our city once shared a story that really struck me. He grew up in a pentecostal church in which people who came to Christ were instructed to "pray through" until they received the baptism in the Holy Spirit. He explained that the phrase "pray through" describes a person's determination to overcome any barrier until he, or she, receives the blessing of God. He stated, "The only problem with many of these people is that once they 'prayed through' to the fulness of the Holy Spirit, *they perceived themselves as through!*" When they experienced the initial infilling of the Spirit, they felt they had then reached the pinnacle of the Christian life and didn't have to seek God any further.

However, when Paul says to "be filled with the Spirit" (Eph. 5:18), the original Greek makes it clear that he means to "be continually filled." The empowering of the Spirit is not just a one-time event, but an ongoing experience that should be evidenced in our lives on a daily basis.

Not only does Paul mention the necessity of being filled with the Holy Spirit, he also specifies some of the qualities that characterize such a Christian: a heart to encourage others with edifying songs; a desire to sing beautiful melodies to the Lord; a lifestyle of thanksgiving; and a submissive spirit in relating to others.

Spirit-filled believers will not perpetually run in place, stuck on an endless treadmill of worry and care. They will overflow with the life of God, and their lives will be earmarked by fruit and gifts that glorify Him and advance His Kingdom.

6

BURNOUT: THE DISEASE OF
THE OVER-COMMITTED

When Kelly became a Christian, she soon realized that many people in her church had never submitted themselves to the Lordship of Christ. Her congregation was more of a social club than a sincere group of believers. In fact, the pastor never spoke about how to know Christ personally. His main focus was on the problem issues of society. He often quoted such well-known personalities as William Shakespeare, Abraham Lincoln, and Winston Churchill, to name a few, but rarely cited references from God's Word.

Kelly, having a concern for the spiritual welfare of the church, got involved in teaching Sunday school, serving on several influential committees, and establishing a visitation program. She was fully convinced that God wanted to use her and so she worked hard for change.

The response to Kelly's initiatives was pretty good at first — she was instrumental in leading several people to Christ and the fulness of the Holy Spirit. The successes she experienced inspired her to branch into new areas of service, and as a result, she pressed herself for increased productivity. Kelly was also frequently called upon to assist when volunteers were needed for special projects. Her fear of letting God down motivated her to accept more and more requests for her time and energy.

A few years went by during which Kelly was still heavily involved in her church. But this was not the same Kelly as before — she was now overcome with fatigue and discouragement. The individuals who had accepted Christ through her influence, one by one, began to depart from the church to participate in fellowships which were more committed to preaching the Word of God. Now and then, Kelly herself considered leaving the church, but she was driven by a strong sense of loyalty and a deep awareness of how much its members needed her.

Even though Kelly's mission had been to change the church — the end result was that she had changed! Rather than continuing as a joyful Christian witness, she had now become worn-out and ineffective. Actually, it was a struggle just to keep her own relationship with God intact. The frantic pace Kelly had been keeping, and the overwhelming demands of her many obligations, eventually drained her spiritually, physically and emotionally. The more she accomplished, the more she realized there was to do. Frustrations mounted; progress was slow. Kelly felt like a failure. In short, she was burned out.

A Closer Look At Burnout

Burnout is sometimes called the disease of the over-committed. It can be defined as "a state of physical, emotional, and mental exhaustion marked by physical depletion and chronic fatigue, feelings of helplessness and hopelessness, and by development of a negative self-concept and negative attitudes toward work, life and other people."[1]

The most zealous Christians (who are expected to carry more than their share of the load in the Lord's work) are usually the most likely candidates to experience burnout. Kelly is a good example of a person who remained a loyal worker in her church even at the expense of her own well-being. Her desire to serve God's people was good, but she did not use the best judgment in allowing herself to become spread too thin to the point of exhaustion. In a similar way, one man, when asked about his walk with the Lord, smiled and said, "I'm just burning out for Jesus, brother!" This is certainly nothing to boast about, for burnout can destroy our Christian witness.

52

Burnout begins with stress. Stress can be defined as spiritual, physical, mental, and/or emotional strain or tension. It can often come into our lives when we go through (or think we must go through) a significant change in our current pattern of life. Marital problems (sometimes leading to separation and divorce), deaths of loved ones, pregnancies, serious illnesses, scheduling over-commitments, job conflicts and similar experiences are all very taxing on us. Going through difficult times such as these is a normal part of life and some of the foregoing situations cannot be helped. Other stressful events, however, can be avoided by making wiser decisions concerning how we use our time.

Medical research has clearly established that unwarranted stress is a major contributor to heart, lung, and other ailments and could even cut short our lives. We must not let this potential threat to our overall health go unchecked. It's the devil's way of stealing productive days from us that could be useful to God.

Kelly's determination to see changes occur in her church was admirable, but the stress of committing herself to so many things was, in the end, devastating to her own spiritual growth. The tremendous pressure she felt to be "the savior" of her congregation was too big a load for her to carry. She became burned out.

How can we recognize the signs of burnout in our lives? The following checklist will be helpful in evaluating our spiritual condition:

1. A sense of failure, frustration and dissatisfaction with our work or ministry.
2. Feeling that no one really cares about us or appreciates us.
3. Perceiving that people expect too much of us.
4. A belief that God demands too much from us.
5. Hopelessness and lack of purpose, initiative or direction.
6. Going through the motions but experiencing a lack of joy or inward motivation.
7. Resentfulness toward our responsibilities and toward those who expect things from us.
8. Having a desire to quit, resign, or run away.
9. Irritability and unkindness toward co-workers, spouse and children (putting them down, blame shifting, etc.).

10. Hypersensitivity to criticism or suggestions.
11. Fearfulness, paranoia, or feeling out of control.
12. Increased difficulty in dealing with sinful temptations.
13. Lack of control of the tongue.
14. Constant feelings of physical or mental fatigue.
15. Inability to relax or cease from our work or worry.
16. Withdrawal from meaningful relationships with others.

Feelings Of Failure

I struggled out of bed one morning, managing a faint-sounding "Hallelujah." Invigorated by a warm shower, I reached for my Bible to have some personal time with the Lord. He had been speaking to my heart recently about my lack of dedication to a regular time of prayer, worship, and Bible study. Then I noticed the clock.

"That's incredible! It's 7:30 already! I've got a meeting with one of the men from church at 8:00," I muttered in disbelief.

When I arrived at the restaurant where we had planned to meet, I found my friend eagerly waiting for me. He wanted to discuss some things that were troubling him, and he wasted no time getting started. All during breakfast, he enthusiastically shared his convictions that we, as Christians, need to be more concerned about helping the poor people of the world. My head began to spin as he recited some statistics about the staggering number of people who are hungry and impoverished.

"I'm just not doing enough to help these people," I thought to myself. "God wants me to wake up and see His love for those who are poor and needy."

By the time I left the restaurant, I was feeling discouraged because I hadn't experienced the same depth of burden my friend felt. Guilt feelings welled up inside me, for in comparison to his intense concern for the unfortunate, it seemed as if I had no compassion at all.

I jumped into my car and turned on the radio, hoping to hear an uplifting word on the Christian station. One of my favorite speakers was preaching about the need to reach the world for Christ. "We have to be more committed to evangelism," he proclaimed, as he expounded on the tremendous amount of sin in our society and the vast number of people who die each year without knowing Jesus as Lord.

"He's right," I agreed. "I certainly haven't been sharing Christ with enough people. How can I be such a hypocrite? I've got to find more time to witness to non-believers!"

I went home around noon, looking forward to having lunch with my wife and children. Linda, in her own gentle way, spelled out all the jobs that were not getting done in the upkeep of our house. "The grass should be cut; the wood on the patio floor is rotting out; the garage needs cleaning..." (and these were only a few of the things she mentioned!). "We need to maintain a good testimony in front of our neighbors, honey," she explained. "God wants us to be above reproach, and I think we should make it a priority to have some immediate improvements around here."

Now I was really feeling depressed! Even though I was trying hard, I still fell short in so many ways. I thought to myself, "I can't wait to get to our Bible study group tonight. I sure could use some encouragement from my friends."

The topic at our meeting that evening was the importance of consistent Christian fellowship. One man declared, "God is calling us to join our hearts together in a deeper way and wants us to be involved with each other's lives daily — not just once a week!"

Another person responded, "That's right. We should be more committed to each other and to know each other's needs on an intimate basis. God wants us to love one another as He loved us."

"They're so right," I silently concluded. "It's been two weeks since I've invited someone over for dinner. It seems I always fail to love other believers as much as I should. Forgive me, Lord. I'll try to find more time to reach out to your people in the future."

I didn't sleep very well that night.

Have you ever experienced days when you felt like a failure in a number of areas of your Christian life? There was no question that the things I had heard were true: quiet times, ministry to the poor and needy, evangelism, fulfilling household duties, and being more committed to other believers were all very important. I knew that I could be doing more to accomplish these objectives. Yet, instead of

55

being encouraged to press on, I felt overwhelmed by the immensity of the needs I was neglecting. In my eyes, I couldn't see anything that I was doing well enough to please the Lord.

I have noticed that I typically respond to situations such as these by first feeling guilty and frustrated. Flooded with the awareness of my lack of fruitfulness as a Christian, I then schedule an overabundance of activities to compensate for my perceived failures. The extra activities exhaust me and my efforts become spread too thin. It doesn't take long for me to feel burned out.

Because I can always find someone who is more involved than I in evangelism, prayer, church acitivities and family life, I'm never convinced that I'm doing enough. But even when I seek to improve my situation by taking on an added workload, I rarely feel satisfied that I measure up to what God desires — there is simply not enough time. Depression is right around the corner and I lose the joy of my walk with Christ. Burnout.

On the other hand, we may respond to our perceived failures in the opposite way. Rather than increasing our workload and pushing ourselves to try harder, we may become apathetic and listless toward God. When all of our best efforts seem to fall short of His will (in our eyes), we may decide not to care. We then immerse ourselves in such things as our jobs, recreation, and family life, turning to them and, at the same time, subtly turning away from a closeness with God. Our church involvement often dwindles, for we dread the thought of hearing another message that makes us feel like failures. Disillusioned and confused, we find no joy in our pursuits and feel as if something is missing from our lives. Burnout.

At this point, it becomes easy to develop the wrong idea that God is harsh, demanding, and impossible to please. We may conclude that it is the Lord who keeps requiring us to run in so many different directions at once, and that He's responsible for all the weighty burdens we carry. Then we question why He demands so much from us when it only causes us to feel guilty, frustrated, and unable to get the job done. Our relationship with Christ goes on hold. Burnout.

We sometimes hesitate to confess to our Christian friends that we have lost our enthusiasm for God, feeling sure we already know what they will say. In times past, we may have advised others to deal with such burned out feelings by "being more committed," and "praying more," and "spending more time in the Bible." And yet, following our own advice doesn't seem to work for us right now. The admonishment that we are *not doing enough* is the last thing we want to hear in this condition! Even if there is some energy left to carry on, we probably have lost much of our vision for the eternal significance of what we are doing. Since during this critical time we tend to doubt God's calling in our lives, we desperately need to be inspired and stirred again by an inward conviction of how He can use us.

Have you left your first love because you felt too much "performance pressure"?

The Way Out

You may find that many of these characteristics of burnout are present in your own life. If so, there are some practical steps you can take to be spiritually revitalized.

First of all, get some time away from your family and friends just to spend with the Lord. You may want to go for a walk or to a special place where you can pour your heart out to Him in an undistracted way. Be honest with God about your misplaced priorities, wrong attitudes, stressful circumstances, overactivity, or whatever else has led to your state of exhaustion. Ask Him to refresh you, to fill you anew with His Spirit and, as you do, commit yourself to obey His will for your life.

The next principle to counteract burnout is to reassess your priorities. Make a list of all the things you are presently doing, focusing on the activities that are a source of stress. You will need to take the offensive, aggressively looking for ways to improve your situation. Some things may need to be eliminated from your schedule entirely — others may simply need to be redefined or adjusted to help eliminate unnecessary pressure. Ask the Lord to show you your sphere of responsibility and avoid taking on tasks that are meant for someone else (II Cor. 10:12-16).

Although there is always plenty of work to be done, God does not expect me, or you, to be a superstar in every area of Christian ministry.

Nor does He want us to feel that the accomplishment of His eternal plan rests solely on our shoulders. In fact, the Lord often wants to teach us to accomplish more by doing less! Through giving up prideful self-reliance, His divine power can work within us and surpass any effort we could generate on our own.

The pressure we feel to complete multiple ministries (all at once) is not from God, but something we either place on ourselves or allow others to put upon us. We must recognize the seasons in our Christian lives, for as Ecclesiastes 3:1 tells us, "There is an appointed time for everything." Just as the earth goes through the various seasons of winter, spring, summer, and fall, so too will we experience times in our walk with the Lord when He will be emphasizing one truth more than others. Rather than overwhelm us, when God speaks He will usually challenge us to grow in one specific area at a time. We must therefore grow in our sensitivity to discern His purpose for us at a given season.

We shouldn't measure the level of our spirituality by the amount of work we're doing for God. Actually, much of the activities we say we're doing for Him may very well be, in reality, *activities for ourselves.* As previously indicated, we often use these efforts as a yardstick to evaluate our maturity in Christ and to determine how good we can feel about our walk with Him.

We hope other people will notice our deeds and commend us for our dedication and willingness to make such sacrifices. If we don't receive this recognition, we may become angry or depressed. Thus, we keep pressuring ourselves in order to prove our worth and significance, while calling this pressure the "leading of the Lord." Rather than face our low feelings of self-esteem (which is getting to the root of the problem), we may just become busier.

In addition to using overactivity to feel good about ourselves, we also hope that our many achievements will convince God how acceptable we really are. But attempting to please Him and gain His favor through our many efforts is an attitude thoroughly *condemned* by the Scriptures! God doesn't require us to work ourselves to death to please Him, and He doesn't want us to get so wound up in our responsibilities that we shut out His leading and burn out.

If we are listening, God is faithful to reveal His principal concerns for us at each season of our lives. He always shows great care, selectivity, and precise timing in the truth He brings our way. We can rest assured that according to First John 5:3, "His commandments are not burdensome." Our Lord gives us enough grace to handle every task He asks us to do, yet we sometimes become needlessly overwhelmed by going beyond our God-given limits. As someone so aptly put it, "The will of God will never lead us where the grace of God cannot sustain us."

The will of God will stretch us, but will never lead us to burnout.

The Master's Priorities

There once were two servants who were competing for the same job, hoping to be employed by a rich and prominent man in their community. The master of the household gave Servant A and Servant B an equal opportunity to get the job by giving each of them a list of ten chores to do.

Servant A was very bright and energetic, and felt confident that he would be chosen by the master. After receiving his list, he enthusiastically approached the first item, which was to wash the dishes. He completed the job quickly and then went on to the next item: dust the television set. As he was doing this, he noticed there was a spot on the carpet that needed cleaning. He took care of the spot, then saw that the windows were dirty and proceeded to wash them. Servant A continued to find more and more things to do, even though they weren't on the list. He was sure that the master would be pleased with his initiative and would hire him.

Meanwhile, Servant B plodded along, doing everything on his list until he had completed every chore the master wanted him to do. When it came down to the final decision, who do you think got the job? One might think it would be Servant A because he did so much more, but if you chose him, you were wrong. Servant B was hired because he was a man the master could count on! Although Servant A was very productive and had done all kinds of worthwhile things, he had hardly done anything on the master's list! By ignoring the priorities that had been entrusted to him and pursuing tasks *he himself* valued, he failed to please the master.

Many people allow their walks with the Lord to wander off in circles. They expend much effort, but make little progress toward any goal. Real fruit and productivity are the results of knowing the concerns on our Master's heart and moving in faith to fulfill them. Producing fruit as Christians requires us to lay down our own expectations of what the Lord wants, and choose instead to listen to Him and obey.

There's no need to feel bad if we find that someone else is doing more than we are. *All we can do is all we can do!* Although everything God speaks in His Word is important, we as individuals can't excel in all the gifts and ministries of the Spirit at the same time. Therefore, let us commit ourselves to fulfilling our Lord's purposes for this season of our lives, while remaining open to the new directions that become evident when the season changes.

Some Christians fail to take time off to rest for their own rejuvenation, since it makes them feel guilty to be involved in something so "unspiritual." But God is a God of rest as well as a God of action. He is the One who gave us the principle of the Sabbath (taking a day to rest each week) for our well-being. He is not opposed to our setting time aside to relax, have some fun, and enjoy some recreational activities. Such things as praying, regular exercise, good sleep habits and reading can help us relax and keep our hearts at peace before the Lord.

As previously indicated, much of the stress in our lives is self-induced, caused by pursuits which exalt us, help us save face, or promote us in some way or another. It often comes from wrong priorities such as seeking to excel in school or our careers to simply boost our own egos; trying to look good to others around us whom we think we need to impress; becoming obsessed with making money to help us feel better about our position in life, etc. We could avoid a great deal of heartache by yielding our pride to God and allowing Him to reshape our self-image so that it is truly centered on Him. By so doing, we will no longer feel the necessity to "be someone" or excel in something just to feel good about ourselves.

God wants to replace our self-centeredness with the security of knowing who we are in Him. Unless we have this kind of foundation, we will constantly experience pressure to look at our achievements and activities as the sole indicators of our Christian growth. If this pattern continues, burnout will eventually come knocking at our door.

Cultivating genuine friendships that enable us to share freely with others will also be a big help. We need the loving support of Christian friends and the accountability that comes from those who love us. Not only can they encourage us and tell us how special we are; they can also speak the truth in love when we need to make some adjustments (Eph. 4:15, 16).

A pastor or Christian counselor could also be of major help to us in making some changes in our lifestyle. Sometimes a third party can be more objective in his (or her) evaluations, helping us to find realistic solutions to our problems.

In any event, we must be diligent to avoid the devastating effects of burnout. As Psalm 46:10 so aptly instructs us: *"Cease striving [let go, relax, be still] and know that I am God."* It's one thing to *serve* God and quite another to try to *be* God! Stressful circumstances and heavy pressures will come. They always do. But, through the power of the Holy Spirit, we can learn to overcome this potential threat to our walk with the Lord.

[1]"Clergy and Stress Burnout," an article by Minister's Life Insurance Company, P.O. Box 910, Minneapolis, Minn., 55440.

7

THE CRIPPLING EFFECTS
OF HABITUATION

Bill isn't excited about God any more.

He's been a Christian for over a decade and has been teaching an adult Sunday school class for the last two years. He is a faithful churchgoer, but the familiar routine of his church and his pastor have left him feeling stale and cold. Bill listens to dynamic sermons about Jesus and feels empty. He listens to the messages on faith and feels untouched. He hears testimonies about the exciting work of Christ and he's — well, bored.

Now, Bill isn't happy about this situation. In fact, he's having a rough struggle with it. He knows something has gone wrong, and he's afraid his heart is drifting away from the Lord. Although Bill longs for a fresh awareness of God, he's at a loss as to what he must do to find it.

What's happened to Bill? He's run into one of the worst barriers any Christian can face in his walk with God: *habituation.*

Habituation is the experience of growing accustomed to something by the process of being continually exposed to it. To explain it another way, it is the act of becoming so familiar with some circumstance or event that the experience of it requires only a second-natured, mechanical response on the individual's part.

Imagine yourself walking into a large industrial plant for the first time. You probably would be greatly annoyed by the clamor of the machines around you. Yet, the factory workers, engrossed in the work they are doing, seem oblivious to the extreme noise of their environment. The workers have obviously become "habituated" to the sound of the machines; that is, they have become so accustomed to the noise level of the equipment that, for all practical purposes, they are able to shut out the noise and not let it affect them. On the other hand, an outsider to the factory routine would be greatly bothered by it.

I can remember when I got into trouble as a youngster, my dad would usually begin his lectures with one of the following two statements: "Bob, if I've told you once, I've told you a thousand times..." or "Bob, a smart man only takes one time to learn." By the time I was a teenager, his point of view had become quite familiar to me, and as a result, my attention often wandered while he was speaking. Dad would begin one of his "sermons" and I would look at him and nod my head, while proceeding to shut out his words from the moment he began his introductory remarks. Since I assumed that I knew what he was going to say before he even spoke, I missed many opportunities to really listen and learn from him.

We tune out noise, we tune out voices; in fact, our tendency is to tune out just about anything we've heard over and over again. It shouldn't surprise us then to realize that, in much the same way, we tune out God.

Perhaps you can identify with my childhood experience of praying every night — as fast as I could —

> *Now I lay me down to sleep,*
> *I pray the Lord my soul to keep,*
> *If I should die before I wake,*
> *I pray the Lord my soul to take.*

We can readily see that after praying this prayer a few hundred times, it's easy to just recite the words in a lifeless way and not really think of their meaning at all. One might wonder how many of our prayer times have been hampered because of the repetitious nature of our petitions and our lack of a flexible, creative response to God.

Shortly after becoming a Christian, I attended a youth fellowship meeting every Sunday night. It was normally expected that we would sing a song called "Pass It On." The youth group had a very limited repertoire at that time, and "Pass It On" was a real favorite. When I first learned this song, it was fresh, alive, and full of meaning for me. Yet, it eventually became little more than a mere repetition of words because I had grown so used to singing it. The beautiful lyrics, once so inspiring to me, could no longer stimulate my spiritual growth because habituation had occurred.

We become habituated not only by what we continually hear, but by what we constantly do. Whether we stand or sit as we worship, lift our hands, recite a liturgy, read the prayers, or kneel on cue, sooner or later these experiences can lose their freshness and vitality. They then become automatic, devoid of a genuine heart involvement.

Recognizing the Danger of Habituation

Maybe you're encountering this yourself — the feeling that all your spiritual efforts are monotonous and fruitless. You wonder how you can keep your walk with God challenging, interesting, and meaningful.

Habituation occurs in much the same way as inoculation works against disease. A doctor will inject a small dose of a disease into our bodies to help us develop an immunity to it. In much the same way, many of us have allowed ourselves to become inoculated against God by experiencing only a small dosage, or a mild form, of His presence and power. Content with this minimal exposure and feeling that this is all we need, we allow "antibodies" of habituation to shut out a closer walk with Him. Satan hopes that we will be satisfied with small glimpses of God and occasional interventions of the Holy Spirit in our lives, rather than the abiding sense of the Lord's presence we are meant to enjoy.

Practicing empty routines and traditions won't please the Lord and won't do much for our Christian growth, either. Nevertheless, thousands of individuals, and oftentimes entire churches, have been stifled by their reliance on religious habits — repeating the same words, the same songs, and the same patterns — instead of allowing God to move them in creative, new directions and bring back the sparkle to their walk with Him. This is when habituation cripples us the most. It causes us to lose our flexibility in being led by the Spirit, since we find it more comfortable to settle back in habit patterns that have worked well in the past, even if they lack the ability to keep us interested now.

Have you left your first love because you've become habituated?

Enjoying the Lord

I can remember a time when a pastor friend of mine asked me to speak at his church. I prayed, sweated, and agonized over the sermon God wanted me to share. After spending hours seeking the Lord for a "mighty message," I still had no direction, no inspiration, and no time left to hunt for it. My brother saw me struggling and complaining and wasn't surprised when I finally griped, "Jim, I'm frustrated! What do you think God wants me to say?"

Jim just smiled at me and said, "Bob, just *enjoy the Lord.*"

I was puzzled — couldn't my brother see that I was in no mood for joking? But as I thought more about it, the truth of his statement hit me like a bombshell. Here I was, making something exciting into a terribly frustrating effort. My whole focus had been on getting something to say that would bless and impress my audience, instead of simply enjoying the Lord and allowing my heart to be at rest before Him so that He could lead me. God *did* want me to speak a word for Him, but this word would flow naturally into my heart if my desire wasn't just to "get the correct message," but to enjoy Him as well.

How easy it is for activities that once were meaningful in our Christian lives to degenerate into mere ritualistic exercises. Whether it be preparing Bible studies, having daily prayer time, attending church functions (all of which are good), it's possible to perform them mechanically without experiencing the joy of the Lord.

Psalm 100:2 tells us to "Serve the Lord with gladness," and "Come before Him with joyful singing." No matter what our circumstances in life, God invites us to live closely with Him and bask in the joy of His presence. As the Psalmist so beautifully proclaims: "In Thy presence is fulness of joy: In Thy right hand there are pleasures forever" (Ps. 16:11).

Being a Christian is not mindlessly responding to a set of religious rituals; it is not simply "doing the do's" and "avoiding the don'ts." It's a relationship to be enjoyed — expressing our hearts with freedom, laughing and having fun together, showing warmth, love, and acceptance, and sharing a oneness of purpose. But many believers don't picture their walk with God in these terms. To them, relating to God isn't a joyful experience. It's work, it's drudgery — it could hardly be described as fun!

For this reason, an important principle in conquering habituation is to seek the Lord for His wisdom on how we can keep our Christian lives from flattening out into a set of dull, machine-like routines. No love relationship can thrive on routine. We get bored too easily. Our attention wanders and we tune out our beloved until the love fades away. The same thing happens in our relationship with God. If our formerly meaningful expressions of love degenerate into futile exercises, then our relationship with Him will become stale. We're not the only ones who feel the dryness: God is not happy with our unimaginative procedures either!

My wife, Linda, has taught me many helpful lessons during the years of our marriage. I have learned that she greatly appreciates variety in our relationship. She isn't satisfied doing the same things over and over, but wants to have special times with me. Among other things, she likes to walk in the park, go to a new restaurant, see a play, ride bikes, go canoeing, or visit close friends. Linda desires our times together to be more memorable than sitting at home in front of the television set, and more varied than attending fellowship meetings every evening. The Lord has used my love relationship with Linda to teach me about Himself — He enjoys having special times with us too!

One thing I like to do is to go outdoors and gaze at the wonders of creation, while filling my mind with thoughts about the awesomeness of God. In these moments, I may remain silent, or else pause to lift my voice in praise, or unload the concerns of my heart. These are some of the most notable times I have ever had with Him. Perhaps you can remember a particular location (a sanctuary, an outdoor setting, etc.) where you experienced a closeness with God in the past. Have you considered returning to that place and pouring your heart out to Him in a fresh, new way? The place, however, is not the important thing —it's the expectancy of your heart and your sincerity before God that makes the difference. Don't deprive yourself of these precious times of undistracted fellowship with Him!

A Vision Beyond Ourselves

An additional help in overcoming habituation is to maintain a vision of how God can use our lives to further His eternal purposes.

Tony was struggling in his walk with the Lord. He knew he should spend time reading the Word, worshiping and praying each day, but it was apparent that he lacked the discipline to fit these things into his daily schedule. In former days, Tony had a deep desire to grow as a Christian, but now his motivation was waning. He seldom missed church, however, and often asked the congregation to pray that he would gain more consistency in his spiritual life.

Seeing Tony's inner turmoil, his Christian friends tried to hold him accountable to a daily routine. They were faithful to ask him how he was doing, and frequently exhorted him to make God more of a priority. The prayers, the numerous exhortations, and the account-ability bore little fruit. He had become habituated.

As Tony and I were talking one evening, it suddenly dawned on us what had happened. He had lost a sense of vision for his life, a vision of how God could use him. His focus had become inward and he was now consumed with taking care of himself and his family.

In his earlier, more motivated days, Tony had been a part of an evangelical church that encouraged its members to reach out to non-believers in an effort to bring them to Christ. At that time, he saw a weakness in his personal evangelism and wanted to learn how to share his faith more effectively and become ready to answer whatever Bible questions he might be asked. Besides preparing to share the gospel with others, Tony was receiving special training to assume a position of leadership in the church.

The vision Tony had — which went beyond just providing for himself and his family — made him acutely aware of his need for growth and became a crucial ingredient in stimulating his daily devotions. His times with the Lord were filled with a sense of purpose and direction. He was convinced that God had planned a special ministry for him.

However, in the years that followed, Tony had experienced many changes in his life — a new church environment, a new home, a new job, two children, and a vision that grew dimmer with the passage of time. Gone was the thrill and sense of urgency he previously felt to prepare for Christian service.

To Tony, life was like a revolving door: going to work, being home with his family, putting in his weekly time at church, only to start the cycle all over again. He still claimed that he wanted to have some daily devotions, but he hardly ever succeeded. Even when Tony did make room for God in his schedule, such times rarely seemed to uplift him.

For the most part, the only thing that did give him satisfaction was knowing he had fulfilled his "obligations" to God, even if the experience didn't seem fruitful. His conscience soothed, Tony would then feel like "a success" that day. In time, the mere fact that he squeezed a few minutes into his schedule for some devotions became an end in and of itself (to help him feel as if he was a faithful Christian), rather than a means to an end — to grow closer to God and do His work on the earth.

No wonder Tony struggled. Proverbs 29:18 clearly states: "Where there is no vision, the people are unrestrained, but happy is he who keeps the law." The word "vision" can also be translated "revelation," and revelation (as discussed in chapter one) refers to God unfolding Himself and His purpose to the human race. Without this vision we become unrestrained, or literally "out of control." The context suggests that people without vision will cast off all restraints and, as a result, fail to keep God's Word. They become undisciplined and cease to follow the Lord's direction for their lives and their happiness departs.

During my college years I was involved with Campus Crusade for Christ and became familiar with their witnessing tool called the "Four Spiritual Laws." The first principle in this booklet is "God loves you and has a wonderful plan for your life." I can remember how excited I was to learn that God had a unique blueprint for me.

Many believers begin their spiritual journeys with the realization that God has a plan for their lives, only to lose sight of this truth after a time. To them, the only plan that unfolds is the "exciting" and "abundant life" of gutting out daily quiet times and pushing themselves to attend a few church meetings each week. There's a whole lot more to our walk with Christ than this! God's purpose is for us to joyfully fulfill a place of Christian service. He is committed to extending His kingdom throughout the earth and He wants us to be His vessels to bring men and women under the Lordship of Christ. This awareness should capture our hearts and inspire us to prepare for the task ahead!

Embracing this wider vision stretches us to be all that we can be for God. It stimulates growth, it rallies us to prepare, it challenges us to let Him use us beyond our wisdom and capabilities. It causes us to trust Him, for unless we do, we run the risk of failing miserably. Someone once said, "If your vision isn't bigger than yourself (i.e., what you can accomplish by your own efforts), it probably isn't from God." He loves to place before us certain opportunities or tasks that can only be acomplished by His provision.

Moses was asked to do something quite impossible for him to do in his own strength — lead the people of Israel out of slavery in Egypt. Joshua was asked to conquer the Canaanites with a group of people who had little military experience. Gideon was asked to defeat the Midianites with just three hundred men by his side. We could go on and on with such biblical examples. Like these men, we too will be called by God to expand our faith and do things beyond our own capabilities.

Are you presently being challenged by a vision beyond yourself? If not, here are some practical suggestions. First of all, confess to God any complacency you have had in your devotional life. He is more than willing to forgive you.

Next, find some time alone with God and ask Him to show you a specific ministry that you can fulfill. It may be an area of service in your church that will be spiritually challenging to you, or perhaps an outreach ministry to unbelievers. Whatever you do, don't be afraid to let God stretch you by placing a vision on your heart that is beyond your present ability to accomplish. He will faithfully equip you to do all He wants you to do!

After gaining some general direction from the Lord, ask Him to help you form these ideas into some concise, practical, and obtainable goals. Write them down and keep them in a place where you'll be reminded of them on a regular basis. Let these goals provide you with specific focus and motivation as you set aside special time for Him.

It is unfortunate that many people who are incredibly goal-oriented in the secular world have no sense of direction or purpose in their Christian lives. Some believers even conclude that setting spiritual goals is ungodly since following them might cause us to lose our sensitivity to the leading of the Spirit. There is no need, however, to place the ministry of the Holy Spirit in opposition to establishing some clear-cut objectives for our lives. Jesus Himself said that the Holy Spirit would disclose to us what is to come (Jn. 16:13). He will place a burning vision upon our hearts for how we can serve in the most fruitful way.

After clarifying our current goals, it would also be good to share them with our pastor, spouse, or some close Christian friends. Their loving input and support can be invaluable to our spiritual progress. How important it is to surround ourselves with those who will encourage us in the Lord!

In the final analysis, the motivation of the Christian life must come from within. Getting down on ourselves for lack of discipline in our devotional life is not the total answer. Relying on the constant prodding of other Christians is not enough. Motivating ourselves because our pastor or other friends tell us we should have daily devotions will not stand the test of time. Nothing can replace God's grace in our lives, a grace that bubbles up from within, a grace that propels us ahead.

And from this grace, God imparts an ongoing vision for our lives —a vision that motivates us to persevere and inspires us to overcome the crippling disease of habituation whenever it appears. This vision must grip our attention and captivate our hearts! Its fulfillment does not rest upon what we can do in our natural ability. He alone can bring it to pass and He delights in using us as His vessels to reach the world.

8

UNFULFILLED DREAMS

There are many people who reach a place in their Christian walk where they catch a vision of how God can use them, only to find that some years down the line, the vision remains unfulfilled. The dreams they once had for effective service eventually became only dim memories.

This is true in the life of a middle-aged woman I shall call Norma. She was convinced that God spoke to her while she was still a child about serving Him as a missionary one day. But much time has passed since then and her desire for full-time Christian ministry is unrealized. Harder yet to deal with is that, in her present circumstances, she sees no way possible to carry out her dream. Her present circumstances include four children, a spiritually unresponsive husband, and a ton of household responsibilities.

Norma's vision and hope that God would fulfill her childhood impression is slowly dissipating. Feeling frustrated and guilty, she often chides herself over certain choices she made in the past, especially the decision to marry her husband and have so many children. "After all," Norma concludes, "haven't my family duties held me back from pursuing my missionary calling? Perhaps I should leave home so that I can be obedient to God's call." Normally she would never even consider such a drastic course of action, but as the years continue to speed by, she experiences a growing urgency to find some way to reconcile her present situation with her earlier vision.

At a time like this, it is easy to forget that God is not limited by that which seems contradictory in our eyes. If Norma is accurate in her childhood perceptions, certainly God would be willing to exert His power to carry out His Word — even if her situation presently looks bleak. Perhaps there are factors in Norma's life (unbelief, disobedience, etc.) which have hindered God from bringing His will to pass. Or, maybe there is a time period later on in which her dream will be realized. The questions are endless — we may have to wait for the answers.

Unfortunately, this kind of questioning process will only lead Norma into fruitless, unhealthy introspection. It would be far better for her to place the leading she thought she received as a child on the storage shelf of her heart, lifting it up to God periodically to see if He would materialize it. If He doesn't work to bring into existence the impressions we receive, then we must not move out prematurely to accomplish them ourselves. Serious consequences can occur when we take matters into our own hands and get ahead of God's timing.

There is a training process for Christian ministry which necessitates gaining knowledge and experience and going through a time of testing and proving in the Lord. As we wait for His timing, we must be humble enough to be whatever He wants us to be. God has no trouble *raising up* gifted people into leadership; His trouble is getting us to *come down* to a place of patient humility!

The Waiting Process

There are those who receive excellent teaching on spiritual gifts and exercising Christian leadership who are initially excited to hear about the tremendous potential they have in the Lord. They project themselves ahead, visualizing years of powerful, anointed ministry —only to find out that five, ten, fifteen years later, little or none of their ministry aspirations were achieved.

Pete, feeling a call to pastoral ministry, was diligent to prepare for it by receiving theological training in a leading seminary. After he graduated, he became a full-time pastor of a thriving, young congregation. Shortly after, he developed some serious financial difficulties which threatened the welfare of his family.

Seeing no way to resolve his financial problems without some radical changes in his lifestyle, Pete stepped down from the pastorate to go into business and pull himself out of debt. In his mind, the change in his occupation was only a temporary transition point until he could get back into his primary field of interest — serving in full-time ministry. After all, being a pastor was what he originally felt called to do and he had invested several years and lots of money preparing for it. Surely God would use him in this capacity again.

Now, years later, Pete still hasn't returned to the pastorate as he had originally planned. A number of medical tests uncovered a serious heart condition that could well be aggravated by the stress of ministry — and besides that, no doors opened for him to lead a church. Even though Pete is making good money now, He is often troubled by the apparent conflict between what he originally felt led to do and the job he is currently doing. With each passing year, more and more doubts creep in concerning God's perfect will for his life.

Perhaps you also are struggling to harmonize your present place in life with the plans you previously envisioned for your future. It once seemed so clear what God intended for you, but now you are confused, disillusioned, and afraid that you may have let Him down. Since your dream has never come true, you wonder if you have disobeyed God at some point, thwarting the accomplishment of His plan.

At times like these, the devil loves for us to get discouraged and reason to ourselves that we failed to obey the Lord completely (by marrying the wrong person, indulging in certain sins, choosing a restricting career, etc.). Or, we may falsely conclude that God has failed us (because He kept us on a string waiting for something that He was neither willing to fulfill nor powerful enough to accomplish).

Either of these reactions can lead to depression and serious spiritual decline. Some even fall away from their original faith because they don't know how to handle this discrepancy.

Suppose we truly have failed God to some extent. God is indeed hurt by our sins and obviously displeased, but He is rich in mercy and forgiveness. He will give us a new start and put us on the right track again. The issue then becomes not how well we have done in the past, but to what extent we are living in the fulness of His Spirit today.

Someone once said, "You can't drive a car by constantly looking in the rear-view mirror!" This is true of our Christian lives as well — we don't get anywhere by placing our attention on the mistakes of the past. Just because we failed to obey the Lord in days gone by doesn't mean we have to permit that trend to continue. If we will open our hearts afresh to the Holy Spirit, He will empower us to walk in the Father's will *today*, and, in His timing, doors of Christian service will open for us.

After we have condemned ourselves over a period of time and have become tired of feeling like a perpetual failure, we frequently will shift the blame to God. We wonder why He hasn't fulfilled His Word, when in reality what He hasn't fulfilled is *our interpretation* of His Word. We feel like a mouse that faithfully pursued a fake piece of cheese.

It is important to realize, however, that receiving impressions from God and interpreting them accurately is limited by the extent of our maturity as Christians. Such things as our emotional state at the time we are seeking guidance, confusing circumstances, and the influence of fleshly desires can also cloud our spiritual perception.

As a result, we may think God spoke something to us and falsely construe its implications for our lives. When a discrepancy occurs between "the promise" and its manifestation, we are then set up for a faith crisis in which we begin to doubt God's faithfulness. Many sincere Christians have found themselves in such a dilemma, unable to reconcile inward impressions of what should happen with the outward circumstances that are actually taking place. In light of this, the Bible assures us that "... the Lord is the One who goes ahead of you; He will be with you. He will not fail you or forsake you. Do not fear, or be dismayed" (Deut. 31:8).

It is also possible that we have heard from the Lord and He is bringing about the answer to the promise in a different way than we ever imagined. One might wonder if Norma's vision (concerning her involvement in missions work) was meant by God to be brought to fruition at a later date. Sadly enough, by following her present tendency toward skepticism and discouragement, she will be impeding

76

her spiritual progress and fail to gain full benefit from this important season of preparation.

God often expects us to let go of *our* dreams and aspirations so He can replace them with His vision for our lives (Isa. 55:9). When I was single, I can remember how God brought me to a place where I was willing and ready to remain unmarried for the rest of my life if that was how I could best serve Him. This was indeed a miracle, since as long as I could remember, I had a desire to be married someday. Soon after I came to a place of inner peace about remaining single, I met a beautiful woman named Linda, who eventually became my wife. The willingness to let go of my expectations and fully submit to Him seemed to be a key in releasing His hand to provide the perfect wife for me.

Overcoming a Spiritual Mid-Life Crisis

In the past decade there has been much said by psychologists and professional counselors about the topic of "mid-life crisis," which is especially common among men. The mid-life crisis usually occurs between ages thirty and fifty and is a time of serious personal evaluation. During this period, the realization that we are indeed getting older generates a host of questions about the value and significance of our lives. Typically a person in a mid-life crisis will be heard making the same basic remarks:

> "I just turned thirty-five and what (money and material things) do I have to show for it?"
>
> "I'm stuck with my present job and there's no room for advancement — what should I do?"
>
> "I thought I'd be a lot further along in my career by now."

There is also such a thing as a spiritual mid-life crisis that occurs when Christians become severely discouraged about the gap between where they think they should be in their growth and where they are in reality. Some of these believers were convinced that God would use them in mighty ways — as evangelists, prophets, miracle workers, etc. Although they are usually five, ten, fifteen (or more) years old in the

Lord, their dreams of a dynamic ministry have not been realized. There is little fruit to show for the many years they have under their belts as Christians. They have blamed themselves and others and even questioned God. As the confusion over the apparent discrepancies in their lives grows stronger, these people will be tempted to slip away from their original faith.

We can rise up out of such circumstances, shaking off the disappointment and apathy, and fasten our eyes on Jesus again. As we let go of *our* aspirations, God will be able to speak to us about *His* desires for our lives. Even when we correctly comprehend the Lord's vision, we must be willing to keep lifting it up to Him for its fulfillment. The timing, the means of accomplishment, and the exact events that bring God's will about may be different than we expected. Nevertheless, we must wait, resting in the knowledge of His faithfulness to bring about His purpose for every committed Christian (Rom. 8:28, Ps. 37:4, 5).

9

DIGGING UP THE ROOTS
OF BITTERNESS

Joan has left the Lord.

She once made a genuine commitment to Him, and actively followed Him until she experienced the greatest crisis of her life. Her mother died after a long, difficult struggle with cancer. Joan was heartbroken and could not understand why God allowed this terrible thing to happen. "How could a loving God let her die?" she asked herself. "It just isn't fair. Mother was so young and she loved life so much!" To make matters worse, Joan's mother had never professed to know the Lord and Joan regretted that she hadn't been a better witness for Christ by taking more time to help her during her suffering.

Joan's pain and turmoil were aggravated because her Christian friends were "just too busy" to reach out to her during this difficult time. She felt abandoned. "Where were my friends when I needed them?" she often complained. Even though Joan tried to resist her feelings of bitterness, the more she brooded about her situation, the more resentful she became toward God and her friends at church.

I have noticed that, almost without exception, people who are estranged from God have become disillusioned because they think He has failed to meet some pressing need or desire in their lives. Perhaps you have felt this way yourself. Have you gone through a painful divorce, or gone bankrupt when your business failed? Have you prayed consistently for a wayward child, only to see him or her get into deeper trouble with drugs, cults, or crime? Have you prayed for the healing of someone dear to you, only to watch your loved one die?

A local pastor was in a similar situation. He used to visit a woman every week who was suffering from what the doctors diagnosed as terminal lung cancer. Over a period of months, and through much prayer, she gained more strength and showed some signs of progress. She got out of bed, dressed, and bought a wig to cover the baldness caused by chemotherapy. Praising God for her recovery, she witnessed faithfully in the hospital to others who came for regular treatments. The pastor was delighted — but suddenly her condition reversed and deteriorated. She failed rapidly and soon died. Reeling from disappointment and confusion, the pastor took his anger to the Lord and asked, "Why? Why did this happen?"

At some point in our lives we all find ourselves looking at God and asking Him that toughest of all questions.

Why?

In Isaiah 55:8,9 we read:

> "For My thoughts are not your thoughts,
> Neither are your ways My ways," declares the Lord.
> "For as the heavens are higher than the earth,
> So are My ways higher than your ways,
> And My thoughts than your thoughts."

And Paul tells us in Romans 11:33-36:

> Oh, the depth of the riches both of the wisdom and knowledge of God! How unsearchable are His judgments and unfathomable His ways!
> *For who has known the mind of the Lord, or who became His counselor?*
> Or who has first given to Him that it might be paid back to Him again?
> For from Him and through Him and to Him are all things. To Him be the glory forever. . . .

In other words, whatever the problem, whatever the disaster, whatever the depth of disappointment, disillusionment or grief, God's wisdom is much higher than our own. In fact, sometimes the only sure answer we receive to the "why question" is this: God knows more about it than we do.

Is this good news? Yes. It is good news because it means the entire situation can rest fully in the hands of the one Person who can understand it perfectly, handle it with absolute fairness, and care about it with flawless, compassionate, unfailing love.

Trusting the Goodness of God

Like Joan, we don't always see anything fair or loving in the distressing events of our lives because we don't see the total picture. There once were two boys who were struggling to watch a parade through a knothole in a fence. A third friend climbed to the top. The two boys at the knothole could see only a small part of the ongoing parade, the part going directly past the knothole. Their friend on top of the fence could see the entire parade. Often our perspective is limited because our experience, too, is similar to looking through a knothole. But God's outlook is far superior: He sees things from a heavenly perspective, knowing both the origin and the conclusion of our experiences, plus everything that will happen in between.

Our Lord assures us that He "causes all things to work together for good to those who love Him and are called according to His purpose" (Rom. 8:28). The word "good" in this verse does not mean having our own way or experiencing a life free from adversity. Rather, it is good according to God's perspective, as defined in the next verse: that we might be "conformed to the image of His Son." God is working in the midst of our greatest difficulties to produce in us a more complete likeness of Christ.

We must look for His guiding hand and His awesome power to be displayed in each and every situation we face, for through great trials come great testimonies! That's right — the men and women in the Bible we admire the most for their faith were all people who saw God work miraculously to bring them through horrendous problems. But how can we be expected to trust God when someone we love is

81

desperately ill, or we are facing financial ruin, or our child is to be tried in Juvenile Court on charges of breaking and entering? Isn't that asking a lot? Yes, it is. But that's exactly what God asks. More than that, it is what He requires of us. We must trust Him!

To trust God during the most abysmal moments of our lives requires us to have a strong, accurate concept of Him, for we can't trust someone who we are not convinced is worthy of our trust. This is the reason it is vital for us to look to the Word of God for our answers, and not to our own understanding and feelings (Prov. 3:5,6). He is faithful to reveal Himself in His Word.

The gospels are a good place to begin — nowhere else in the Scriptures are we given such a loving picture of our Lord. As we follow Jesus through His earthly ministry, we will see Him moved with compassion and reaching out to the poor and heartbroken. We will observe Him as the Good Shepherd who willingly laid down His life for us, His sheep. We are touched by His tender heart in forgiving the woman caught in adultery, and in receiving the little children who came to Him so freely. And we will learn that Jesus, in all His gentleness, kindness, and love, reveals to us the character of God the Father. In John 10:30 He tells us, "I and the Father are one," and in John 12:45 He says, "And he who beholds Me beholds the One who sent Me."

The One who sent Jesus is our Father God, our Dad, whose steadfast love inspired the Psalmist to sing:

O Lord, my heart is not proud, nor my eyes haughty;
Nor do I involve myself in great matters,
Or in things too difficult for me.
Surely I have composed and quieted my soul;
Like a weaned child rests against his mother,
My soul is like a weaned child within me
(Ps. 131:1, 2).

What a precious picture this is of the type of relationship the Lord wants us to have with Him! When we put aside all our fears, our doubts, our nagging questions "why," and put our trust in Him, we can

82

climb up into His arms and rest against Him like a little child. Surely Joan needed to do this, but she didn't. Many people don't.

It is not uncommon to build our expectations about God around our own desires, around what we want Him to do in a given situation. We conclude that because we are Christians, we have a right to have everything go smoothly. However, there will be times when our perspective of what is best will not even resemble the way God chooses to operate! This occurs, not because our Lord is capricious, but because His ways are often too far above our capacities to comprehend. These periods of conflict are dangerous for those who aren't walking closely with the Lord, or for those who have not yet learned to trust His promises in the Scriptures.

When we hope that God will work in a particular way, and He doesn't, discouragement will be knocking at the door. Satan will attempt to play upon the frustration we feel to convince us that God doesn't really care and can't be counted on to fulfill His Word. He will try to deceive us into thinking that God has changed and has revoked His promises so that they don't apply in our particular situation . This is nonsense! It is absolutely contrary to the Word of God (Mal. 3:6; Heb.13:8). Even so, it is astonishing how many Christians cope with a crisis by listening to these lies, all the while allowing disillusionment to crush their relationship with the Lord.

Have you left your first love because He didn't perform the way you thought He should?

Three Levels of Forgiveness

Am I telling you that Joan had no reason to be upset? Of course not. Her mother's death was a harrowing experience and her Christian friends plainly failed her. That's not the point. Like Joan, we will *all* go through difficult trials and struggle with others who neglect or abuse us (I Cor. 10:13). It is our *response* to these situations that is the issue with God.

We are instructed in Hebrews 12:15 to "See to it that no one comes short of the grace of God; that no root of bitterness springing up causes trouble, and by it many be defiled...." As we can see by Joan's experience, if we entertain anger in our hearts and allow it to develop into full-scale bitterness, we will be pulled away from a close walk with God and head for a rapid spiritual decline.

Suppose that a root of bitterness has sprung up. What can we do about it?

God told us what to do about it. In Mark 11:25, Jesus instructs us:

> And whenever you stand praying, forgive, if you have anything against anyone; so that your Father also who is in heaven may forgive you your transgressions.

And in Matthew 6:12,14:

> And forgive us our debts, as we also have forgiven our debtors....For if you forgive men for their transgressions, your heavenly Father will also forgive you.

How does this apply to a person like Joan? Joan had a problem on three levels: she was angry with God, she was angry with herself, and she was angry with her Christian friends. She allowed her anger to grow into resentment, springing up into a root of bitterness that drove her away from the Lord and her church. Since forgiveness is the way God instructed us to deal with bitterness, Joan needed to forgive on three levels.

Forgive God?

Yes, forgive Him.

I'm not suggesting that God is ever at fault for any calamity that strikes us. I'm not telling you that God deliberately hurts us, neglects us, abuses us, or torments us. God is absolutely sovereign, and His character, as revealed through His Word and through Jesus (the Word made flesh), is totally incapable of malice.

But when we become bitter against God, we must deal with it. He has done nothing that needs to be forgiven, but by forgiving Him, we willingly let go of the bitterness that has driven a wedge between us. In so doing, we are released from the bondage of resentment that has severed our relationship with the Lord.

Forgiveness is a decision, not a feeling. If it were a feeling, we would rarely forgive anyone! When we are hurt, our tendency is to want to hurt in return and forgiveness is the farthest thing from our minds. For this reason, God, in His wisdom, put forgiveness in the form of a *command* to be obeyed.

We have a clear choice: we can make a decision to respond to God's command and forgive, or we can choose to disobey Him and suffer the consequences. Our feelings have nothing to do with it. It is solely an issue of obedience. Forgiveness restores our relationship with God, giving Him the opportunity to go to work in our lives to bring our emotions into line. Unforgiveness, on the other hand, forms a barrier between ourselves and Him that can only be bridged when we "tear up the I.O.U." we are holding against the other person (Matt. 6:14, 15; 5:23, 24; I Pet. 3:7).

Have you left your first love because you are bitter toward Him?

Forgive God. Make the decision to get free of the paralyzing bondage of resentment. Make the decision to trust Him in all things and accept the sovereignty of the One who knows all, can do all, and cares infinitely about you. Your forgiveness will put you back in touch with Him, and give you the power you need to move on to the next step: forgiving yourself.

Remember Joan's feelings of failure? She felt guilty because, to her knowledge, her mother wasn't a Christian when she died and Joan couldn't remember ever explaining the gospel to her. Joan was not only convinced that she had failed her mother, she was afraid she had also failed the Lord. Joan needed to forgive herself.

Forgiving yourself may be the most difficult thing you ever have to do. It seems that no one is as violent a tormentor as we are to ourselves. Our own personal standards of justice often exceed the requirements of God! "Well, I think God has forgiven me of my sins, but I just can't forgive myself," you might say. I have heard this said many times as I have counseled over the years.

Even though the Bible teaches we will be forgiven by acknowledging our sins to God, it somehow seems just too simple (I Jn. 1:7,9). We may feel we must also suffer in some way for our transgressions. It is natural to experience guilt feelings after we have violated the principles of God's Word and our personal standards. Satan loves this.

In Revelation 12:10 Satan is referred to as "the accuser of the brethren," and he lives up to his title! He is determined to play on our inner sense of failure and get us bogged down in feelings of inadequacy and dejection. He would like to have us running in circles all of our lives, punishing ourselves for those things we have said or done that make us feel guilty.

When God told us not to let the root of bitterness spring up, He meant for us to uproot it *wherever* it emerges, and that includes our bitterness against our own selves. His answer is forgiveness, which He does not suggest but demands, and He expects us to forgive ourselves as well as others.

Again, it's an issue of obedience, not of feeling, and when we decide to obey, we release God's power in our lives to soothe and heal all the damage we have done with our own relentless self-hatred. When we disobey, we leave the rift between ourselves and God gaping open, and we will not only suffer from our negative self-esteem, but also from our increasing estrangement from God.

Have you left your first love because you haven't obeyed His commandment to forgive yourself?

Forgive yourself.

Joan had an additional problem: she was bitter toward her Christian friends. It might seem that after forgiving the sovereign King of the universe and forgiving ourselves for the monstrous debt we owe to Him, forgiving other people would be a simple matter. It isn't. Forgiveness is never a simple matter. It's for this reason that God had to make it a requirement for our lives.

In Romans 12:18 we are told, "If possible, so far as it depends on you, be at peace with all men." Oh, the wonderful grace of our Lord, who does not ask us to do the impossible! He requires nothing of us that He can't enable us to do. All that He asks is that we do everything we can to live in harmony with others. If they don't reciprocate by responding to our initiatives in a positive way, then we can move ahead with a clear conscience toward God, knowing that we aren't the reason that the relationship remains severed. By learning to rely on the grace of our Lord Jesus Christ, we will have the power — His power

—to forgive others who have hurt us and walk in appropriate behavior that reflects God's love rather than harmful retaliation.

The Road to True Forgiveness

You may be wondering if it is possible to forgive someone and still continue to feel upset when you think about the specific situation. Along with making a firm decision to forgive, we must replace our painful thoughts with positive ones. Otherwise, the root of bitterness will find a fertile ground waiting to nurture it again.

First, we should focus our attention on any good points to be found in the situation, asking the Lord to make us aware of those we might have (even deliberately) overlooked.

Second, we should follow Paul's exhortation in Philippians 4:4, 8 to "rejoice in the Lord always" (for He will see us through), and to set our minds on whatever is pure, lovely, and true, etc. When we do this, we will counteract the negative thoughts that often creep in and lead us to become bitter again and seek revenge.

Third, we must allow the Lord to replace our hurt feelings with love for those who have injured us. Only He can do this, and He will, eagerly, if we ask Him to and allow Him to work in our hearts.

Have you left your first love because your bitterness towards others has cut you off from Him?

Forgive them. God will help you. He will move heaven and earth to answer a prayer for His help in forgiving.

Remember that it was He who came into the world on our behalf to heal us of all our emotional scars. Jesus truly understands and feels compassion for us, knowing full well the heartaches and pain we are experiencing (Heb. 2:18, 4:15). He will gladly turn our lives around if we will let Him! "When someone becomes a Christian, he becomes a brand new person inside. He is not the same any more. A new life has begun!" (II Cor. 5:17 TLB)

God's Word never promised that our Christian walk would be free from tribulations, but we are given a most blessed assurance that, through Christ, we can persevere and overcome each threatening circumstance. Jesus said, "Here on earth you have many trials and sorrows; but cheer up, for I have overcome the world" (Jn. 16:33,

TLB). Even today, this same Jesus, who is alive in us, will help us through the difficulties we face as we stay in right relationship with Him and submit to His wise and loving sovereignty.

May our risen Lord be so fully present in our lives that we are able to see things from His limitless perspective, forgiving ourselves and others, even as He has forgiven us.

10

HURTING CHRISTIANS

Although Lisa had once been very enthusiastic about Christ and her church involvement, she no longer wanted anything to do with Christianity. She had been taking an overload of courses at a local university as well as working two part-time jobs to support herself. Because of her crowded schedule, she missed a few months of mid-week meetings and a number of Sunday services.

Several people from the church were upset by her irregular attendance, and one person (who scarcely knew her) called to criticize her for having "messed-up" priorities. Lisa's name was even mentioned at the weekly prayer meeting by someone who asked the congregation to pray that she would "return to the Lord and get free from Satan's control." Not one of these "concerned Christians" showed her any compassion or asked if there was anything they could do to help. Lisa felt belittled and condemned. She could have accepted their words of caution much easier if they had inquired about her personal life or her relationship with God. Instead, they seemed far more concerned about her attendance record.

Greatly embarrassed and bewildered by all that happened, Lisa felt uncomfortable about returning to her church. Her heart ached for someone to understand — for someone to care enough to check out the facts, rather than make all kinds of wrong assumptions.

Lisa's decision to quit going to church altogether further reinforced the suspicions of many in the congregation that the devil had deceived her and pulled her away from God. People freely expressed disdain at her "unrepentant condition" — but no one bothered to visit her to see what was really happening in her life. The only correspondence she received was a periodic letter expressing the financial needs of the congregation and an envelope to receive her absentee contribution. Deeply wounded in her spirit, Lisa eventually concluded it was much easier to live out her walk with the Lord without other believers around to complicate things.

Perhaps you can identify with Lisa's story. You sincerely want to live for Christ, and yet you have been hurt in relationships with other professing Christians who have either cheated you, lied to you, ignored you or otherwise mistreated you. You find yourself being somewhat of a loner. Even though you desire to be close to God, you are extremely disillusioned with the process of being close to other believers.

Rather than going to church each week, you sit at home, lounging around in your bathrobe, alternately reading the newspaper and taking a peek at some of the Christian broadcasts. Vivid memories of previous hurts crowd into your mind, and you tell yourself, "There's no way I could ever get involved with a church group again." In your understanding, the perceived benefits of such involvement aren't enough to outweigh the emotional risks you would be assuming.

We can easily sympathize with Lisa and feel sorry about the way she was treated, but her method of handling the situation (by withdrawing from other believers) was unfortunate and potentially devastating. The Bible commands us not to forsake the assembling of ourselves together for fellowship (Heb. 10:25).

Ideally, Lisa should have expressed her hurts to the pastor in an effort to clear up any misunderstanding and avoid a bitter departure. In an endeavor to find effective solutions, all possible attempts at a reconciliation should have been explored. Then, if the communication process reached an impasse, and Lisa was certain she did all she could to resolve their differences, she should have prayerfully considered asking to be released from her existing membership to find another church home. Complete withdrawal from other believers is not the biblical answer.

Just because Lisa had one bad church experience doesn't mean that all other Christians would treat her in the same way. In fact, in her situation, there were several evangelical churches nearby, any one of which could have provided an excellent atmosphere for her Christian growth. But Lisa wasn't open to it.

Called to Walk Together

Some people boast that they "love God and that's all that really matters," or quip that they "love God, but it's God's people they can't stand!" They don't see a need to become involved in a fellowship of Christians. To them, church involvement is a bunch of headaches and heartaches and not a blessing for their lives. Bad experiences have convinced them that they would be better off "going it alone." However, this type of attitude is destructive and contrary to the Lord's intention for our lives.

Genuine Christianity is not loving Jesus while isolating ourselves from His people. In fact, an important way we demonstrate our love for Him is by showing love to other believers (Mk. 12:28-34; Jn. 14:15, 13:34, 35). We may think we can stand alone without Christian fellowship and be able to fulfill God's highest purposes for our lives, but this isn't so. The Bible tells us that "God has placed the members, each one of them, in the body, just as He desired" (I Cor. 12:18).

The first-century church "continually devoted themselves" to the apostles' teaching, *fellowship*, the breaking of bread, and to prayer (Acts 2:42). Joining ourselves to a church fellowship and fulfilling a role in the body of Christ is not optional — it's a necessity. The part we play is vital to the whole, for *everybody is somebody in Christ's body!*

Larry Tomczak addresses this issue as follows:

> Pressures mounting in our increasingly paganistic society are alerting us to the fact that we can no longer 'go it alone.' We need a shared life ... a community ... a spiritual family. Not in theory but in reality. We need to be joined to brothers and sisters having an all-consuming commitment to follow Jesus and be a living expression of His body on a daily basis.[1]

It is God's intention to unite us in strong relationships with other believers, for our mission is to glorify Him and we can accomplish this objective more completely when we work together. One person's light can illuminate the darkness to a small degree, but a *"city [of lights] set on a hill cannot be hidden"* (Matt. 5:14). Each person's contribution, cheerfully given, creates the total effect of strengthening the church so it can fully establish God's kingdom locally and throughout the world (Eph. 4:11-16).

Knit Together in Love

As a relatively new Christian, I was excited to find a church that was alive in the Lord — a thriving, dynamic fellowship that exalted Jesus Christ and saw many people brought to the saving knowledge of Him. What a time we had as we made it a weekly priority on Sundays to shake hands or hug those seated around us, and tell them how much we loved them. In fact, we even had a special song, "He Is My Everything," that served as our cue to begin greeting those who were seated around us.

From an outsider's point of view, we looked like a tight-knit congregation with a great deal of love and commitment to each other. You would think that a church such as this would be able to weather almost any storm, since it seemed to be built on a solid, Christ-honoring foundation.

And yet, in one evening's time, the church was split over a dispute that called into question the pastor's morality. At least half of the people left the church. Tempers flared, gossip abounded, resentments flourished — the pressure of the moment had brought out some rather ugly attitudes. It grieved my heart to see how seemingly mature believers were reacting to the situation. Where was the love of God in all this?

Paul states in Colossians 2:2: "...that their hearts may be encouraged, having been *knit together in love,* and attaining to all the wealth that comes from the full assurance of understanding, resulting in a true knowledge of God's mystery, that is, Christ Himself." This Scripture suggests that we can only obtain the full wealth of Christ as we become joined together with other Christians in love. We may not find this process of involving ourselves in a fellowship of believers as being an easy one. After all, there is no such thing as a perfect group of people. Disagreements will occur, interpersonal conflicts will creep in that need to be resolved, and some may even treat us in an inconsiderate manner.

Perhaps you, like Lisa, have thought at one time or another, "I don't need all the hassles I get from others. I could be a much better Christian without them around!" This perspective would be right if we defined "a better Christian" as one who never got frustrated, angry, or hurt. But God's perspective is different. He uses the misunderstandings and the tough times we encounter with others to help us grow in Christ. We must therefore press through the hurts and frustrations of the past and find a group of believers to whom we can commit ourselves.

The question we must confront is: do we know how to deal with interpersonal conflicts in a godly way? Disagreements with others often bring out the worst in us — and this insight, although quite painful, is necessary to make us aware of our need for further growth. The inadequacies we feel, when handled properly, cause us to cling to the Lord and find in Him an abundance of love and grace to initiate reconciliation. As we are faithful to obey the teachings of the Scriptures on handling broken relationships, we will become more mature as Christians (e.g., Matt. 5:23,24, 18:15-35; Rom. 12:18; Eph. 4:1-3, 25-32; Col. 3:12, 4:6).

Experience teaches us that Satan's fiery darts are often targeted at discouraged, isolated believers. In fact, many of the cults prey upon these disenfranchised believers who once genuinely encountered God, but who are now all alone, nursing wounds from clashes with His people. With their bruises still smarting and their hurts still present within, the enemy may be able to sow seeds of fear (of close involvement with others) and deception (you don't need God's people to be a "good Christian").

Yet, in all this, God's Word tells us, among other things, to love and encourage one another...to get involved in a church fellowship...to devote ourselves to Christian service...to glorify God as lights to the world. Unless we heed these admonitions of the Scriptures, we will be living contrary to the revealed will of God. We are then prime candidates for spiritual decline, for it is impossible to walk closely with Him when we are clearly ignoring His purpose for our lives.

It is time for us to lay our hurts and disappointments down at the feet of Jesus so that He can rekindle love in our hearts again. His love looks beyond the faults of others to see their underlying needs. God's love casts out all our fears (I Jn. 4:18). His love is full of grace and compassion, and causes us to open our lives once again to the precious believers with whom He would surround us. God's love motivates us to keep trying, to press through differences, and most of all, to love others even when they don't love us.

[1]Larry Tomczak, "You Need to be Committed to a New Testament Fellowship." Tract. For reprints, write People of Destiny, Box 2335, Wheaton, Md., 20902.

11

YOUR CHRISTIAN FELLOWSHIP: HELP OR HINDRANCE?

Pam grew up in a small town in Pennsylvania and had very few friends during her teenage years. Although she longed for companionship, she was very shy and fearful of rejection. She felt as if she never measured up to the expectations of her parents and peers and assumed that no one really liked her.

After graduating from high school, Pam enrolled in a state university some distance from her home in hopes of becoming an elementary school teacher. But the college scene completely overwhelmed her: the big campus, the demanding academic load, the unfamiliar faces, the noisy dormitories — all were difficult adjustments. Fighting through some severe depression during her first semester, Pam often felt like quitting school and going back home.

Later that year, Pam met some people from Campus Crusade for Christ who reached out to her and showered her with love. She was deeply touched by their genuine concern. After hearing the gospel several times, Pam eventually prayed to receive Christ into her life and began going to all the Crusade activities at school. She loved the singing, the fellowship, the hugs, the emotional support, and the listening ears. Every spare moment she could find, Pam sought out her Christian friends. In fact, she rarely was apart from them.

After graduating from college, she moved back home and became a teacher in the same school she attended as a child. Her parents and other family members were not professing Christians at the time, and neither were the other people she knew in her town. Gone was the support of her campus fellowship group. Gone were the days when it was easy to locate other believers and gain encouragement from them. And gone were the happy people who regularly "pumped her up" in the Lord.

Pam is now going through a difficult time. She feels empty and alone without the support of her Christian friends. Sadly enough, her relationship with Christ had become synonymous with her involvement in the Crusade group. She had become close to a number of people —but she had failed to come close to God. There is presently very little happening in Pam's walk with the Lord.

While the desire to build close relationships with other Christians is certainly to be commended, unfortunately there are some who will become more dependent on the people in their particular group than they are on the Lord. For example, when we have a problem, we often go immediately to our pastor or Christian friends for guidance, financial support, personal counseling, companionship, etc., rather than first consulting the Lord. This tendency to rely too heavily on other believers to meet our needs can actually limit what God will be able to say and do in our lives. The Bible exhorts us to "stand firm" *in our own faith* (II Cor. 1:24), and that "each one shall bear *his own load*" (Gal. 6:5).

Instead of becoming familiar with God's leading, we find it easier to consult with others to see if the majority supports our own preference. Or, we may be satisfied to find even one person to agree with what *we want* to do. Upon finding such a person, we then rejoice that God has given us unmistakable confirmation of His will!

True, it is much easier to take a public opinion poll of what our friends think we should do, but they should never become a substitute for bringing a matter directly to God. We can't derive much personal growth if we fail to first consult the Lord for His direction in the matters at hand. In fact, many harmful results can occur in our lives if we automatically interpret the approval of others as being approval from God.

When we make a church fellowship our source and our supply in an unhealthy way, we rob God of much of the glory He deserves. People may indeed be God's instruments or vessels, but He alone is the source of all blessings! (Jn. 3:27; Phil. 4:19; Jas. 1:17) And yet, it is important to be open to the encouragements and rebukes of other Christians; the Lord may be speaking to us through them. We must not, however, become so dependent on others that our capacity to receive guidance from Him is never allowed to develop.

God is presently shaking everything that can be shaken to reveal whether our lives are built on sand or the solid rock of Christ (Heb. 12:25-29). The people who are just hanging around the church will fall flat on their faces in the midst of difficult circumstances. Their foundation won't support them in perilous times because it is based on following Jesus for the personal benefits involved, rather than on a genuine, life-long commitment to Him (Matt. 7:24-27). It is no wonder the Scripture warns: "But the Spirit explicitly says that in later times some will fall away from the faith..." (I Tim. 4:1). Jesus had already expressed this thought by saying: "And at that time many will fall away and will betray one another and hate one another" (Matt. 24:10).

If our individual lives are anchored in Christ, we will be able to stand strong until the end. It is vital, of course, to be committed to a group of believers who can be an important source of encouragement to us.

Motions or Devotion?

Rick had attended a large denominational church off and on for many years, but he had never experienced a personal relationship with Jesus. The born-again experience was simply never talked about in a positive way. There were occasional references to "fundamentalist Christians," although they were usually given in a sarcastic tone.

During his college years, Rick lost interest in attending church, believing it to be irrelevant to his life. However, a few years after graduation, while listening to a Christian radio broadcast, Rick accepted Christ as his Lord and had a sincere desire to follow Him. He was greatly excited about returning to his church, expecting it to have new meaning for him. But his enthusiasm was short-lived.

Rick noticed that most of the people seemed to respond to items on the church bulletin or in the hymnal in a mechanical way, evidencing little or no outward expression of joy. Even though he was a brand-new Christian, he recognized that there was much more to worship than just going through the motions. The apathy he saw each time he attended the Sunday services depressed him.

Eventually, Rick approached the senior minister and expressed his concern. The minister, annoyed at being asked about the congregation's spiritual condition, stated that he was satisfied with the church. He continued by saying, "Not everyone feels as strongly about Christianity as you do. If you're not careful, you'll turn people off by your fanaticism." Rick felt wounded inside. Where were the genuine believers who shared his joy in the Lord?

Some churches foster an atmosphere that caters to those who, for one reason or another, are not interested in growing closer to God. The congregation is never challenged to make anything more than a passive response to Scriptural truth. Often the order of worship is repetitive each week, allowing the people to become so accustomed to responding the same way at the same time that their hearts and minds are scarcely involved at all!

In these churches, the words we say and the songs we sing have little impact on our lives because we have learned to do them routinely. Since we feel we know what is expected of us, we can tune out words and truths that once might have deeply affected us. The result? We become more like professional churchgoers than devoted worshipers. Although we attend church, we never allow our hearts to experience a closeness to God. All the while we deceive ourselves that He is happy with our efforts. The truth is, He's not.

> Because this people draw near with their words
> And honor Me with their lip service,
> But they remove their hearts far from Me,
> And their reverence for Me consists of tradition
> learned by rote . . .
> And the wisdom of their wise men shall perish,
> And the discernment of their discerning men
> shall be concealed (Isa. 29:13,14).

Although the people of Isaiah's day had given lip service to the Lord, their reverence for Him consisted of duplicating "traditions learned by rote." The word "rote" means routine or repetition carried out without understanding, or mechanically done. In other words, performance of their traditions had blinded them to what was really important — having their hearts sold out to God. The sad fact is that they were unaware of how far they had strayed from God's purposes. Isaiah was called by God to warn them of this unfortunate course.

Someone once said, "The seven most destructive words in church history are 'We've always done it this way before.' " The people of God like to "camp out" in situations that are familiar to them. Contemplating change and opening the door to what is new and unforeseen can create a real challenge to our faith and be very threatening. But there's a danger in keeping the church rigidly structured, thereby cutting off the spontaneous moving of the Holy Spirit. The resulting habituation will be a negative influence on the spiritual lives of the people.

As suggested in chapter 7, corporate habituation can occur in each of the events observed in Christian worship, such as praying the Lord's prayer, sharing in communion, reciting the Apostle's Creed, and so on. The greatest hymns and Christian songs throughout the ages, when sung over and over again in our churches, may lose some of their impact on us. In fact, *any* activity that is done on a regular basis without variation will eventually become a mere mechanical exercise for most people.

We should also be aware that we can become unresponsive to the sermon if it is given by the same person each and every week. As we become familiar with our pastor's main points of emphasis and his overall preaching style, we may be able to anticipate what he will say even before he makes his point. Since we assume that we know what his message is going to be, we easily tune out his words and then complain that we're not getting anything out of what he is saying! As a result, thousands of Christians aren't getting spiritually fed in their churches, not because the pastor is failing to speak God's Word, but because the congregation has grown "dull of hearing" (Heb. 5:11).

Habituation in Less-Structured Fellowships

Some churches have rejected a formal liturgical structure in favor of a more spontaneous worship service during which people are allowed to contribute testimonies, Scripture readings, and spiritual gifts. In an attempt to counteract what they perceive as staleness in the institutional church, they assume they are not subject to the ills of habituation because their people have been filled with the Holy Spirit and see the gifts of the Spirit occurring in the meetings. "We don't follow the leading of man — we let the Spirit lead us," some will say.

Although the desire to let the Holy Spirit lead is admirable, there often can be a great amount of repetition in these churches even when there is no written schedule of events. In effect, the congregation may still be confined to a rigid order of worship, although it is simply a part of their memory and their experience rather than expressed in a bulletin. In such services where there is no predetermined order of worship, the unwritten expectations of the pastor, or the people, will "structure" what will happen in the meetings. This invisible structure (fixed by the attitudes of those in attendance), can act as a barrier to the intervention of God among them. The God who longs to come near to us is then kept at a distance, and the church inevitably suffers.

As an example, I was a part of a college Christian fellowship for four years which never passed out a bulletin. In spite of this, we could expect the same order of events to occur each week: twenty to twenty-five minutes of singing; about twenty minutes of sharing (by the same three or four people each week!) and a thirty-minute teaching. The people who attended the meetings could easily predict the songs, the people who would share testimonies and prayer requests, and even what the main speaker would emphasize.

After awhile, our times together lost their freshness, giving way to spiritual staleness. Gone was the anticipation that God would intervene in our meetings. We sang some good songs, prayed some good prayers, and spent time studying God's Word. Even so, something was missing. Habituation had set in and our activities had become more mechanical than spiritual. Our routines came more from our minds than our hearts and, as a result, we missed out on some potential opportunities for growth.

Maintaining Spiritual Vigor

Whether you are involved in a traditional worship service or a church environment that is less structured, habituation is a deadly force that can squeeze the life out of your worship experience. If you find yourself in a church that stifles you in expressing your heart to God (because of rigidness and lack of meaningful variation), it may be time to prayerfully consider whether or not you are in the right one.

Does the Word of God come alive to you? Are you growing in your ability to receive guidance from the Lord? Does the worship uplift you, helping you to experience the presence of God? Do testimonies abound of the life-changing power of Jesus Christ? Are you given the freedom to express a meaningful gift or ministry in the church?

If you are in a church fellowship that isn't helping you to grow in the above areas, it's important to seek the Lord for guidance! If God has led you to your particular church, you can count on His grace to be abundantly supplied to enable you to fulfill your responsibilites. On the other hand, if you still find yourself constantly struggling to maintain a vibrant Christian life, and you have seen little or no fruit in your contribution to date, then something is wrong! It's time to step back and reevaluate.

There are many well-meaning, Spirit-filled Christians (like Kelly in chapter 6) who have spent years of their lives trying to introduce reform in their traditional churches. They pray, serve on committees, teach Sunday school, organize special programs, and do whatever they can to change the system. The unfortunate experience of so many is that instead of changing the practices of their congregations, they themselves become changed.

Many of these people have become discouraged and burned out through overwork and the frustration of seeing so little response to their efforts. Rather than appear disloyal, they continue in their labors, even if their own walk with Christ is steadily declining. And yet, how can they be useful in building God's kingdom if they no longer have a fresh, life-giving relationship with Him?

If we are certain that the Lord wants us to be involved in a specific fellowship, we have no right to blame the church for any spiritual decline in our personal lives. We too often make accusations against other people to cover up our own failure to grow in our love relationship with Jesus. Many believers move from one fellowship to another every few years, never really satisfied with any church they attend. What they fail to see is that often the root problem of their discontentment is their own unfulfilling walk with the Lord.

If we have never learned to deal with personal habituation and sin, we may well sense a need for a new environment to break out of our monotonous routines. The atmosphere of the new church might temporarily shake us out of our current spiritual decline. But unless something changes in our lives, the cyclical process will reoccur and we will become dissatisfied again.

You May Need More

You may find that the services in your church seem to stifle you in worship and hinder you from receiving adequate nourishment in the Lord. Perhaps you could check out some other opportunities for fellowship with others in the congregation who share your interest. A small group Bible study or prayer meeting might be a helpful addition. If your church doesn't already have such groups, you could discuss this with your pastor or an appropriate person in leadership. Maybe you already know some Christian friends who would be excited about participating in one.

Sometimes in smaller and more personal home settings there can be a mutual encouragement and accountability that isn't available in a larger gathering. The flexibility of such a fellowship makes it possible for us to express our hearts to the Lord and to one another without the more constricting patterns that are often imposed in larger church groups.

To sum up, we should not condemn our church for our own failure to have a meaningful and vibrant walk with Christ. Criticalness and blame shifting will only divert our attention away from God as our source. No matter how good our church is, we will have to guard against the ever-present tendency to succumb to habituation and replace our spiritual vitality with just going through the motions.

12

LAYING ASIDE EVERY ENCUMBRANCE

> Therefore, since we have so great a cloud of witnesses surrounding us, let us also *lay aside every encumbrance, and the sin which so easily entangles us,* and let us *run with endurance* the race that is set before us, fixing our eyes on Jesus, the author and perfecter of faith... (Heb. 12:1, 2).

Carl is an alcoholic. As hard as he tried, nothing seemed effective in bringing his drinking problem under control. Then he accepted Jesus as his Savior. Knowing that, as a Christian, he needed to give up his old lifestyle, he sincerely repented and asked the Lord to help him overcome his addiction. His prayer was answered and Carl stopped drinking! His entire life began to improve. Grateful for the things God had done for him, Carl freely witnessed to others about the grace and power of Jesus Christ. He began with an excellent start — but then he made a dangerous mistake.

Carl decided that the best way to reach his non-Christian friends with the gospel was to meet them on their home territory. He began to go regularly to all his old hangouts (bars, of course!), so his former drinking buddies could see for themselves how much he had changed. His friends did not understand why he wouldn't give in and have a beer with them. They pressured him mercilessly. Carl remained strong for several weeks, but he began to rationalize, "It can't hurt to have just one beer as long as I don't get drunk. I'm sure God wouldn't mind." One compromise led quickly to the next, and soon Carl was trapped again in his previous drunken condition.

"What happened?" Carl wondered. "I thought God would protect me and give me power to overcome temptation. I was serving Him faithfully, taking His message to my friends so they could get their lives together — now I'm right back where I started. I feel terrible about being so hypocritical. But where was God's help during this time?"

Where was God all that time? Right there. He was beside Carl every moment, and His will pertaining to drunkenness was clearly stated in the Bible Carl was carrying around. But he stopped looking to God for help in conquering his drinking habit, and so he stumbled. The key to victory over sinful habits is plainly given in the Word of God. Tragically, Carl didn't seek it out.

Does this mean Carl wasn't born again? No, it means that he stopped too soon. Like those who receive Jesus as Savior and never take another step, Carl stopped in his tracks and tried to live off the strength of one experience. The sad fact is that many new believers, as well as many old-timers in Christ, have never learned to overcome their habitual sins.

In Ephesians 2:1, Paul described the lives of those without Christ by saying, "And you were dead in your trespasses and sins." Sin, which is missing the mark of God's perfect will, forms an obvious barrier between a person and God. By saying that we were *dead* in our sins, the Apostle is proclaiming that we, as non-believers, were cut off or separated from our only source of life, the Lord Jesus Christ (Jn. 14:6; I Jn. 5:11,12).

Furthermore, each one of us inherited a selfish, sinful nature that influences us to please ourselves instead of making God's desires our highest concern (Rom. 5:12-21). Paul gives us the following instructions in Ephesians 4:22-24:

> that, in reference to your former manner of life, you
> *lay aside the old self* which is being corrupted in
> accordance with the the lusts of deceit, and that you

> be renewed in the spirit of your mind, and *put on the new self,* which in the likeness of God has been created in righteousness and holiness of the truth.

The "old self" refers to our basic nature (outside of Christ) that is bent toward selfishness, covetousness, arrogance and the like. The words "lay aside" in this passage are found in the aorist tense of the Greek language, conveying the idea of a past action occurring at a distinct point in time. Paul, then, is sharing with us that there should be a decisive, clear-cut, once-and-for-all putting aside of the old self.

The imagery that Paul is using in the above verses is taken from putting on or taking off a garment. But he is not speaking of a superficial change in a believer's life or a so-called conversion experience that is external only. The aorist tense of the original Greek suggests a permanent laying aside of the old garment — **never to be worn again!**

Thus, Paul is challenging the Ephesian church to become permanently severed from the dominion of sin by actively "putting on" the qualities of Christ, which he describes as the new self. As long as they hung onto their old way of life instead of relinquishing it to Jesus, they would continue to fall prey to their own lusts of deceit (Eph. 4:22). Paul exhorts them to diligently pursue the only avenue that would lead to victory — making a "clean break" from the corrupt nature that held them captive.

Shortly after becoming a Christian, I became involved in a Bible study with some friends of mine from school. We didn't realize it then, but the teaching we received was unbalanced, continually stressing God's grace and His desire to forgive our sins, to the exclusion of other important spiritual truths. No mention was made of God's hatred of sin and His desire to liberate us from sin's power.

As a result, we began to accept the erroneous notion that the only way to deal with our habitual sins was to repeatedly ask for forgiveness. Feelings of guilt and helplessness were our frequent companions. We wanted our lives to change, but wrongly believed that the ever-present influence of our sinful nature would make victory virtually impossible. Not knowing of God's offer to give us power over sin, we lived defeated lives — sinning, asking forgiveness, and sinning some more. We were caught in a perpetual cycle that we seemed powerless to overcome. As frustrations mounted, our initial love for God began to fade.

Have you left your first love because you have been unable to break free from sinful habits?

We are Crucified with Christ

Perhaps you are saying, "I've tried to live a godly life, but I just can't seem to control myself." Or, "The harder I try to be different, the more I seem to mess up." A vast number of believers struggle with these kinds of thoughts. Is there something we have overlooked in our presentation of the gospel of Jesus Christ? I think there is.

> For you have died and your life is hidden with Christ in God.
> When Christ, who is our life, is revealed, then you also will be revealed with Him in glory.
> Therefore *consider the members of your earthly body as dead* to immorality, impurity, passion, evil desire, and greed, which amounts to idolatry (Col. 3:3-5).

In Galatians 2:20, Paul continues along this line:

> *I have been crucified with Christ;* and it is no longer I who live, but *Christ lives in me;* and the life which I now live in the flesh I live by faith in the Son of God, who loved me, and delivered Himself up for me.

These verses make it clear that God's goal goes beyond just improving our outward appearance; He desires to do a work of transformation deep within. I am reminded of a man who was trying to fix up his old jalopy. He knocked out the dents, put on a new coat of paint, laid some carpet on the floor, and polished the vinyl seats. But all of his efforts made little difference because he still couldn't get the car to run!

Simply renovating the exterior of our old jalopy (our sinful way of life outside of Christ) does not satisfy Him — He wants to bring a whole new car into existence! All the patch-up work in the world will not change our fundamental nature. We need a new beginning! Since God intends to bring forth something new, the old car should be tossed in the junk heap.

So many people are struggling to gain a sense of consistency in their Christian experience and to escape the paralyzing effects of their pasts. They fail to realize the sufficiency of Christ's work on our behalf. And they fail to live in an ongoing awareness of the crucifixion of our old selves with Him. The cross of Christ not only provides cleansing for our sins, but it also is the means for us to gain freedom from the ungodly domination of our sinful nature.

The Bible says that "...*by His doing* you are *in* Christ Jesus," which is a description of our intimate union with Him (I Cor. 1:30). The term "in Christ" fills the New Testament and is particularly prevalent in Paul's writings. By placing our faith in Jesus, we become "united with" or "identified with" His work on our behalf (I Cor. 6:17). Therefore, when Jesus died on the cross, we who are one with Him also died. That is to say, our old selves, spiritually speaking, were nailed to the cross, and by this great act God delivered us from the very power of sin. He struck a deathblow to our old nature by crucifying it in the eternal sacrifice of Christ. We must embrace this truth with our whole heart, believing it to be true regardless of the mistakes of the past, and accepting it as reality even when our feelings tell us something different. Let's look at this principle applied in three different ways: death to sin, the Law, and the world system.

Death to Sin

God's solution was not to patch up our old nature and make it look better, or to ignore it, by just patiently forgiving us when we mess up. Instead, He threw it on the junk heap, choosing rather to start over again with a brand-new life fashioned after the likeness of Christ. Thus, His method of bringing us out of slavery to our sinful passions is not just to forgive us when we do wrong—He gets to the heart of the problem by both *crucifying* and *burying* our old selves (Rom. 6:4; Col.2:12).

But that's not all that our Lord has done for us. When Christ was raised from the dead, we too were raised to "newness of life," having had His resurrection life imparted to us (Rom. 6:4). *We have been given* a new nature that not only wants to do God's will, but is fully capable of doing it! (II Cor. 5:17; I Jn. 3:1-10) The death to our old nature has allowed for the replacement of our human frailty with the power of Christ's dynamic life! By living out of what we are "in Him" (as opposed to living out of our own wisdom and strength), we have the capacity to turn away from sinful temptations and walk in all that God wants for our lives.

Even so, we occasionally hear about people who, claiming to be born again, persist in their former lifestyles and insist they're doing it "for the Lord." A stripper preaches the gospel while she bumps and grinds. A drug pusher proudly tithes his income from the illegal sale of cocaine. An unmarried couple lives together, testifying that God has blessed their union. A homosexual publishes a book praising the Lord for helping him "find his true sexuality." An alcoholic insists that God keeps him addicted to alcohol so he can preach to other alcoholics with "true understanding." However, we cannot sin to the glory of God! (Rom. 6:1-7) The results are ludicrous. Our Lord can't be manipulated to fit into a framework of sin.

According to Ephesians 2:6, God has "... seated us with Him in the heavenly places, in Christ Jesus." The ascension of Christ was His ultimate glorification. His position at the right hand of the Father bears witness to the fact that "all power and authority" are His, and that "every knee" shall bow to Him (Matt. 28:18-20; Phil.2:9-11).

Knowing that we are seated with Christ gives us the utmost peace of mind. For He is not anxiously biting His nails, wringing His hands, or nervously pacing the floor. He is enthroned in the heavens with the knowledge that all His enemies will one day become a footstool for His feet (Ps. 110:1; I Cor. 15:25). This means that the One who reigns supreme over the universe now reigns supreme over the committed Christian.

Our problem is that we often remain oblivious to His guidance and fail to trust in His sovereignty over all the circumstances we encounter. Yet there is no obstacle too great, no situation too big for us who are in Christ to handle. He, who has all power and all authority in the universe, has made it available to us in the mighty infilling of the Holy Spirit. Upon His ascension, Jesus baptized His disciples in the

Spirit, and this divine enabling is still vital for our Christian lives today (Acts 1:4-8; 2:38,39).

Recognizing the completeness of Christ's work and its implications for our lives is very important, but the Word of God takes us one step further. Galatians 5:16 states that if we "walk by the Spirit," (which means to walk under the Spirit's control), *we will not "carry out the desire of the flesh."* The moment-by-moment influence of the Spirit helps us to "catch ourselves" when temptation to sin arrives, and gives us the strength to overcome it.

The foregoing truths about our union with Christ can be summarized as follows:

1. We were once dead (as non-believers) in our transgressions and sins (Col. 2:13; Eph. 2:1,5; Rom. 5:12-14, 6:23).
2. Now we are *dead* to our previous life outside of Christ (Col. 3:3-5; Rom. 6).
3. We were *buried* with Him in baptism[1] (Rom. 6:4; Col.2:12).
4. We were *raised* up with Christ from spiritual death (Col. 3:3; Eph. 2:6).
5. We were *seated* with Christ in the heavenly places (Eph. 2:6).

The work of salvation that Jesus performed was for you and me! He was our substitute over two thousand years ago, and because of all that He has done, we can presently enjoy, in a very real sense, a spiritual union with Him. This is the liberating truth that Carl missed. This is the life-giving teaching my Bible study group lacked. Victory over sinful habits begins with this realization.

"Habits" can be defined as learned patterns of behavior that can either be helpful or destructive. They develop as we respond to something physically, mentally, or emotionally a number of times. When we form habits, we lock ourselves into certain response patterns that tend to resist change. Most research suggests that the brain never really forgets a habit, although it may drop out of dominance through lack of use or by being replaced by a stronger one.

We must admit that sinful habits are difficult to overcome because, after awhile, we begin to perform these behaviors automatically, with little preceding thought. I have noticed that unless I become angry at a particular habit that is holding me in bondage, I have a difficult time shaking loose from it. When we become angry at our sin, we are motivated to channel our attention in one direction — solving the problem (Heb. 1:9; Ps. 101:3).

There once was a little girl who got her hand stuck in a cookie jar. She tried and tried to pull it out, but it just wouldn't budge. She began to cry hysterically, and her parents quickly greased her hand with butter and corn oil, yanking it until it became red and sore. As a last resort they broke the jar, only to find that the little girl had been grasping three large cookies. "Why didn't you let go of the cookies, Patty?" her parents asked. She answered, still sobbing, "Because I want to eat them!" In much the same way, we claim that we want to be delivered from the inconveniences of sin, but we sometime refuse to let go of the cookies!

Although it may take time to form new habit patterns to replace the old ones, by uniting our will with God's will, the Holy Spirit is free to work in our hearts to bring forth the desired change. One thing we can't do is to hide behind the "I can't help it" excuse, for we *can do all things* through Christ who strengthens us (Phil. 4:13).

Death to the Law

Attempting to earn righteousness (a right relationship with God) on the basis of our good deeds is perhaps the most subtle of all sins. In Romans 7:1-6, Paul expresses concern for those people who seek to gain God's favor through self-effort and law-keeping. The analogy he uses is a powerful one. Speaking primarily to Jewish Christians at this point (7:1), Paul tells them that they were once married to the law and were bound to uphold all its obligations. Yet now, in Christ, they have become dead to the law and are thereby free from the demands of the original covenant. The severance of the old relationship has provided an opportunity for these believers to be married to another, that is, to Christ Himself.

Human effort, born out of our own pride, will never be good enough to merit a righteous standing before God (Isa. 64:6; Phil. 3:9). James 2:10 states: "For whoever keeps the whole law and yet stumbles in one point, he has become guilty of all." The law demonstrates to us that we are guilty sinners and shows us the impossibility of justifying ourselves before a God of perfection. It also points out our need for God's grace.

110

So many Christians today wallow in feelings of self-pity and discouragement because they perceive God as someone who constantly demands more than they are presently giving. The awareness of their repeated failures has cast doubt on whether God's promises will ever materialize in their lives. No matter how hard they try and how much progress they make, they eventually assume that God wouldn't be satisfied with them anyway. Feelings of hopelessness then crowd into their minds and they become vulnerable to satanic attack.

Upon receiving the gift of Christ, we must lay aside all further attempts to merit His favor through our own efforts. Such efforts are offensive to Him and stifling to the foundation of faith that is critical to our spiritual growth. Basing our closeness to God on our up-and-down feelings or on our performance (or lack of performance) of good deeds is a mockery to the cross of Christ. As Galatians 2:21 states: "I do not nullify the grace of God; for if righteousness comes through the Law, then Christ died needlessly."

Thus, righteousness cannot be obtained through obedience to the law; it only comes through faith in the finished work of Jesus. As Paul so beautifully articulates, our whole life is now lived *"by faith in the Son of God,* who loved us and delivered Himself up for us" (Gal. 2:20). In Him, we have full assurance that we are acceptable in God's eyes! (Rom. 10:4; I Cor. 1:30; II Cor. 5:21)

Death to the World

Jane had been an enthusiastic Christian for several years, but now her zeal for the Lord seemed to be diminishing. One day she chatted with my wife and me and admitted that she was undergoing a difficult time in her walk with the Lord. Not only had she fallen into sexual immorality, she had also begun to question whether she could trust the Bible as a guide for her life. She claimed she was in the process of "revamping her Christianity," and urged us to remain open-minded as she went through this "time of searching."

As we listened to Jane, we were deeply concerned. She had become captivated by secular psychology and was beginning to look to humanistic writers for her answers rather than the Lord. Jane eventually concluded that evangelical Christians were too rigid in their standards; they made people feel guilty for their imperfections, and were intolerant of those who disagreed with them. Several months later, she withdrew from fellowship with other believers and departed from her original faith.

Jane's story is like that of many others who have been detoured in their Christian walk by the philosophies of the world. We are heavily bombarded with billboards, movies, television, books, magazines and newspapers which advocate a totally different lifestyle from the one God wants for our lives. Our society would like to convince us that we can get along quite well without God. The fact is, we can't.

Have you left your first love because you have been influenced by the lusts of the world?

Colossians 2:20 states that we "... have died with Christ to the elementary principles of this world...." And yet, our adversary, the devil, is waging a fierce war to control the mind and heart of the Christian through getting us to buy into the worldly values of our society. Since our value system dictates our overall approach to life, it isn't surprising that our enemy concentrates his attacks in this realm.

However, those of us who are in Christ don't have to be controlled by the evil activities of Satan. Through the power of the Holy Spirit, we can successfully resist the enemy's attack and render him powerless to dominate our lives. It will be necessary, however, to consider ourselves crucified to sinful lusts, ridicule, rejection, discouragement, condemnation, and the like, which are some of the weapons most frequently used against us. Overcoming these forces by faith, we can move ahead to accomplish the will of God.

Knowing that our lives are "hidden with Christ in God" and that we are shielded by His mighty armor (Col. 3:3; Eph. 6:10-20), we can face the future with confidence. The Bible tells us that this perverted world system is passing away (I Jn. 2:17) and that Satan is a liar and a defeated foe (Col. 2:15). As someone once said of him, "The devil *promises everything,* but *delivers nothing* of value to us."

Putting on the New Self

Going back to Ephesians 4, let us look carefully at verse 23: "And...be renewed in the spirit of your mind...." Has your mind been transformed by the dynamic power of the Word of God? Do you see yourself as crucified with Christ, yet now made alive by His resurrection power? (Rom. 8:10-14)

God has called us to walk in a clear conscience before Him.[2] This means that as soon as we recognize that we have erred in our thoughts and actions, we must confess our sin to God and repent (that is, turn away) from all that is unpleasing to Him (Lk. 13:3; I Jn. 1:5-10). Repentance may be synonymous in our minds with "banging ourselves over the head," or experiencing intense feelings of depression over personal failure. However, this perspective by itself is woefully inadequate.

True biblical repentance always leads to the assurance that we have no existing barriers between ourselves and God. It is accompanied by the joy of a restored relationship, the joy of the prodigal son coming back to the Father's waiting arms (Lk. 15:11-32). Repentance is more than a one-time event upon our conversion to Christ — it is an ongoing activity that needs to occur whenever we become aware that we have sinned.

Therefore, when the Holy Spirit speaks to us and our conscience informs us that we have erred, we must make a decision. We can either repent and obey the Lord and receive the joy of knowing His complete acceptance. Or, we can give "the devil an opportunity" to gain a foothold in our lives (Eph. 4:27). Like Carl, some Christians foolishly flirt with temptation by getting as close to it as they can without *really sinning*. They are asking for trouble! The Bible warns us to "... put on the Lord Jesus Christ, and make no provision for the flesh in regard to its lusts" (Rom. 13:14).

If we are honest with ourselves, we are usually aware of the areas in our lives that are the most vulnerable to sin. When we determine that we have an Achilles heel in some area, we can then take preventive measures, carefully guarding the entrance-way of our hearts from wrong influences. Our conscience, renewed by the truth of God's Word, can be an invaluable help to us, since it alerts us to improper motives and attitudes even before they are expressed in outward sin. We might compare this to detecting cancer in its early stages — it is easier to find a successful treatment when the disease has not spread too far.

Paul continues by saying in Ephesians 4:24: "and put on the new self, which in the likeness of God has been created in righteousness and holiness of the truth." Again we see the aorist tense in the Greek used to describe the decision to (once-and-for-all) put on the new self. By taking this step of faith, we can replace our sinful habits with the new lifestyle of righteousness, holiness, love, and so forth, that is ours in Christ (Col. 3:5-17).

Perhaps you, like Carl and Jane, and the members of my old Bible study group, are struggling today in your Christian experience. You may have come to Jesus with a distorted understanding of what the gospel is all about. This could be the reason you are not currently experiencing the abundant life that Jesus promised (Jn. 10:10). The good news of the gospel is that we can come to Christ and die to those things that have held us in bondage — sin, self-righteousness, and the evil world system!

Coming to Christ means an end to life *on our terms* (for those who are dead can't make any further plans). It means a complete surrender of ourselves to Him! Through relying on His Spirit, we can say "no" to sin in our lives. We are delivered from constant guilt and frustration over uncontrolled thoughts and actions. The tyranny of sinning and sinning again will then come to a decisive end and we become free of the encumbrances that hinder our Christian growth. We learn to live in victory!

[1]The significance of water baptism is often greatly underemphasized. It is a command of Jesus for every believer (Mk. 16:16; Matt. 28:18-20). Baptism by immersion is an important visual demonstration of our union with Christ in His death, burial and resurrection. In the baptism of the Holy Spirit, we become identified with the ascension of Christ and are empowered for Christian service (Acts 1-2; 8:9-24; 9:1-19; 10; 11:15-18; 19:1-6).

[2]The human conscience is a God-given part of our essential make-up. It is an inward judge of right and wrong; a voice that speaks from the heart to tell us if our thoughts, motives, and actions are consistent with our value system.

13

SPRINTING TO THE FINISH LINE

"Runners to your mark, get set, **go!**" The gun went off with a resounding bang and two runners began the most challenging race of their lives. The two contestants could hardly contain their excitement over the privilege of competing in this prestigious event. It would not be an easy race, they knew, for there were many stumbling blocks and distractions along the way. Even though the course itself was straight, it was so narrow that many athletes had been unable to remain on the track. Some had quit before the race was over, drained of the energy they needed to make it across the finish line. This race required intense discipline and training, and many who had run were unprepared to make the sacrifices needed to succeed.

Don, the first runner, began by sprinting as fast as he could since he believed this was a race of speed. It was not long before he began to grow weary. Although he had started out at a quick pace, he was unable to sustain it. Soon he was running more and more slowly until he was moving at what could only be described as "a snail's pace."

Despite his exhaustion, something kept driving him onward. Several times he felt like quitting, wondering whether the grueling race was even worth it. He knew some of his friends had run this course and given up, overwhelmed with frustration and discouragement. Nevertheless, Don mustered up every ounce of determination within him, steadfastly refusing to fail. He was tired, disillusioned, and rapidly losing heart, yet the race had barely begun. Would he make it to the finish line?

Sandy, the second runner, had realized right away that this would not be a race of speed, but of endurance (Heb. 12:1). She was careful not to exhaust herself during the early part of the race, knowing that she was facing a very long and difficult course. She ran at a steady pace, gliding along with what seemed to be superhuman strength. Sandy was determined to be a winner! No obstacles or distractions would hold her back.

When she heard the great throng of spectators cheering from the grandstands and realized that the end of the race was in sight, Sandy kicked into high gear and began to sprint to the finish line. Although many runners had tried and failed, she not only completed the race, but far exceeded all ordinary expectations, finishing out with a burst of fresh stamina and speed.

In Second Timothy 4:7, the Apostle Paul likened the Christian life to an athletic contest. He states: "I have fought the good fight, I have finished the course, I have kept the faith . . . ." Could you picture your relationship with Christ in the story of Don and Sandy? Many believers have done well in the beginning phases of their Christian walk and are initially filled with enthusiasm to run the race as fast as they can. But God is not only interested in our getting off to a good start. He wants us to be able to build up momentum as we see the end of the race in view.

The race we run is not without a goal. There is a prize to be won. Paul states in First Corinthians 9:24: "Do you not know that those who run in a race all run, but only one receives the prize? Run in such a way that you may win."

What is the prize? What is waiting for us at the finish line?

It's Time to Get Ready

There are a number of Bible teachers who extol the virtues of the present-day church in America. They focus their comments on the success and prosperity the church seems to be experiencing and on the millions of professing believers in our country. They herald the power of Christians to unite together politically to carry out social reform. Even though we can rejoice in the increased visibility level that the church enjoys in this hour, there is still a great deal more that God has in mind.

God wants to purify us as a people for Himself. He wants to rid us of all unrighteousness so that we can reflect His holiness in every area of life. He wants to make us people that can exert a positive influence on our decaying society. Sadly, however, it is sometimes hard to tell the difference between the church and the world. The sins that are so common in the population as a whole (marriage breakups; sexual immorality; addiction to pornography and lust; worldliness; broken relationships; and much more) also abound in the church as well.

And yet, many of us have remained callous toward these developments. We have become numb to the sin in our midst and seem oblivious to how it is hurting our walk with the Lord and our relationships with other believers. There is little fear of God anymore (Prov. 3:7, 8:13, 16:6).

As Peter said: "... it is time for judgment to begin with the household of God" (I Pet. 4:17). There is a definite shaking that is taking place in the church today. God is bringing the sin of our hearts to the surface and exposing the hypocrisy that has hindered us. Hebrews 12:25-29 says it best:

> See to it that you do not refuse Him who is speaking. For if those did not escape when they refused him who warned them on earth, much less shall we escape who turn away from Him who warns from heaven.
>
> And His voice shook the earth then, but now He has promised, saying, "YET ONCE MORE I WILL SHAKE NOT ONLY THE EARTH, BUT ALSO THE HEAVEN."
>
> And this expression, "Yet, once more," denotes the removing of those things which can be shaken, as of created things, in order that those things which cannot be shaken may remain.
>
> Therefore, since we receive a kingdom which cannot be shaken, let us show gratitude, by which we may offer to God an acceptable service with reverence and awe;
>
> for our God is a consuming fire.

God's purpose in allowing this shaking is to remove the things in our lives that are displeasing to Him and devoid of eternal benefit. He wants to establish an unshakable kingdom composed of grateful people who serve Him with reverence and awe. When our God, who is a "consuming fire," moves by His Spirit across the world, there will be a burning away of the remaining vestiges of sin in the body of Christ and painful changes will be required of us. A holy God will settle for nothing less than a holy people! (I Pet. 1:15,16) With this in mind, we must not resist the Lord's dealings in our lives. Do not refuse Him who is speaking! (Heb. 12:25)

A Cry for Revival

The Lord has been speaking a word across our country and throughout the world about preparing ourselves for another significant move of His Spirit. Although thousands were saved during the revivals of the past decades, there is a growing expectancy of something even greater to come.

Many of us automatically associate the word "revival" with special meetings that have been held in churches to win souls and stir up the congregation's zeal for the Lord. But the revival that God wants to bring to His people is much, much more than an event we can schedule on the calendar. His desire is to bring about a visitation of His Spirit upon the earth in unparalleled proportions, sweeping countless numbers of individuals into His kingdom.

Intercessory prayer groups have been crying out for God to bring forth an awakening that would usher in the great day of the Lord. Christian leaders around the world, and especially those with a prophetic voice to the church today, have been sensing that we are on the brink (or perhaps in the early stages) of a mighty move of the Spirit. How we need such a stirring among God's people today!

A defeated, faltering church can do little to further God's purposes. **Christians who have left their first love will not be in the mainstream of what God will be doing in this final hour.** Jesus prophesied in Matthew 24:14 that even though tribulation would abound, the church of the end times would be strong and healthy enough to carry the gospel into all the world. He also instructs us in the same chapter to watch expectantly for His coming (Matt. 24:42-44). "The end of all things is at hand...," First Peter 4:7 states. And James agrees by saying, "You too be patient; strengthen your hearts, for the coming of the Lord is at hand" (Jas. 5:8).

As God moves to purify His people today, let us never lose sight of His ultimate intention. He is preparing us for a marriage celebration! One day Christ, the Bridegroom, will return for us, His bride without "spot or wrinkle" (Rev. 21:1-6, 9-11; Eph. 5:27). The bride/bridegroom analogy helps us realize that God's goal is **not just to visit us** — His desire is to **dwell with us** forever and ever! (II Cor. 6:16-18) Understanding this wider vision of what God is after motivates us to keep our love for Jesus strong in the midst of our degenerating society.

Even though there are a lot of unanswered questions about the direction of society and what is in store for the future of the world, one thing is certain: life on this planet will one day cease to run on a downhill course. Christ will return to dispel all sin and darkness from the earth. For the Christian, there will not be any suffering in the world to come, no depression, no broken relationships, no sickness or pain. Christ will be our all in all, and the place He is preparing for us will be glorious! Jesus gives us a precious promise in John 14:1-3:

> Let not your heart be troubled; believe in God, believe also in Me.
> In My Father's house are many dwelling places; if it were not so, I would have told you; for I go to prepare a place for you.
> And if I go and prepare a place for you, I will come again, and receive you to Myself; that where I am, you may be also.

Fixing Our Hope on Him

Where is your hope today? Is it in yourself and in your own strength to finish the race? If so, you are on shaky ground. First John 3:3 says, "And everyone who has this hope fixed on Him purifies himself, just as He is pure." Our hope should be fixed on Jesus alone to give us the vitality to not only finish the race, but to pick up momentum as we approach the time of His appearing. Picking up momentum does not mean working harder or getting busier for Jesus. It does mean that our love for Him is ever growing and our joyous enthusiasm for following Him never fades away.

By keeping in view Christ's coming and His ultimate triumph over sin, sickness, and death, we will receive a present motivation to press on in our walk with Him. Paul states in Philippians 3:13,14: "...but one thing I do: forgetting what lies behind and reaching forward to what lies ahead, I press on toward the goal for the prize of the upward call of God in Christ Jesus." No matter how far we have progressed in our Christian lives, there is still more room for growth. The "upward call of God" must be pursued. Roadblocks and difficulties will constantly appear to distract us, but we will not be moved when our eyes are upon Him!

When Jesus returns to earth, it will not be as a meek and lowly suffering servant. Rather, He will appear as a reigning and conquering King who will bring all men before Him in judgment. Jesus is not coming back for a church crawling on the ground, exhausted and barely able to continue. He is returning for a church that is "on the alert" and fully prepared to meet Him face to face (Matt. 24:42-51).

It is sometimes hard to imagine how God is going to raise up a glorious church in these last days when so many are either falling away in worldly pursuits or stumbling with fatigue before they reach the finish line. Many Christians are losing impetus instead of gaining fervency and energy for God and His kingdom. But this does not have to discourage us, for our hope is not in ourselves, but in Him.

Because the Apostle Paul understood this principle, he could endure severe hardships for the sake of the gospel. In Philippians 1:6, he gives us these words of assurance: "For I am confident of this very thing, that He who began a good work in you will perfect it until the day of Christ Jesus." Paul could look at the churches of his day and see their immense problems, but still have a positive vision of what God was going to do.

He continues by saying, "...it is God who is at work in you, both to will and to work for His good pleasure" (Phil. 2:13). And to the Thessalonians, Paul writes, "And we have confidence in the Lord concerning you..." (II Thess. 3:4). Peter likewise encourages us in the upward call of God with these words: "...the God of all grace, who called you to His eternal glory in Christ, will Himself perfect, confirm, strengthen, and establish you" (I Pet. 5:10).

Knowing the fact of Jesus' coming, the prophetic call to prepare ourselves for the greatest revival the world has ever seen, and the wondrous promises of God's provision for His people, we can move ahead with complete confidence. For in the fulness of time, according to His eternal puposes, God will bring to pass all that has been promised in His Word concerning His Church.

Do not lose heart or grow weary, but instead, catch a vision of the ultimate triumph of Christ. He is our starting point and our finish line. We can run the race just as Sandy did, with a good start and an exciting finish, sprinting to the finish line with all of our hearts.

Jesus is our prize!

PRACTICAL SUGGESTIONS TO ENHANCE OUR DEVOTIONAL LIVES

Appendix A

Improving Our Study of God's Word

1. *Ask the Lord to personally speak to you through His Word.* Each time you open your Bible, consider it an opportunity to get to know God. What a privilege! Unless you see Bible study as a time of intimate fellowship with the Lord, it will eventually become dull and ritualistic.

2. *Approach each passage of the Scriptures as if you have never read it before.* Cleanse your mind of all preconceived ideas and let the Word speak afresh for itself.

3. *Beware of reading for speed.* You can never tell which passage the Lord wants to use to speak to you, so be willing to pause and meditate on even the most familiar verses. He may surprise you.

4. *Use a variety of approaches.* You could approach your study as a book study; a character study; a word study (tracing a word's usage throughout the Bible); a commentary study (comparing the opinions of various scholars on certain verses); or a theme study (studying a particular theme throughout the Scriptures). Varying your approach in accordance with your current interests and needs will rekindle your enthusiasm, and allow you to escape tedious routines that keep you shut off from God's additional insights.

5.*Use more than one of the well-respected translations.* Using the same translation day after day can become an obstacle if you become so familiar with the wording of a passage that you tune out the new meaning the Lord may want to reveal to you. By comparing the most accurate and respected versions of the Bible, you will get a clear picture of the real meaning of any passage.

6. *Prayerfully ask yourself some pertinent questions.* Paul E. Little, in his book, **How to Give Away Your Faith**[1] lists seven questions that helped him profit immensely from his Bible study time. They will be helpful to us as well as we search for meaning in God's word.

    a. Is there an example for me to follow?

    b. Is there a sin for me to avoid?

    c. Is there a command for me to obey?

    d. Is there a promise for me to claim?

    e. What does this passage teach about Jesus or God?

    f. Is there a problem or difficulty to explore?

    g. Is there something in this passage that I should pray about today?

[1]Paul E. Little, *How to Give Away Your Faith* (Downers Grove: Intervarsity Press, 1966), pp. 124-128.

PRACTICAL SUGGESTIONS TO ENHANCE OUR DEVOTIONAL LIVES

Appendix B

Improving Our Prayer Lives

1. *Vary your posture.* The Bible does not teach us that there is one correct posture in which to pray. We may kneel, bow, sit, stand, walk, fold our hands, lie on the bed, or prostrate ourselves on the floor. The important thing is to use a variety of positions which will allow for greater alertness and attentiveness to God as we pray. On occasion, we all struggle with tiredness which tends to destroy the quality of our times of prayer. By varying our posture, we will avoid assuming such a comfortable position that we become drowsy (Ez. 9:5; I Chron. 17:16; Ex. 34:8; I Tim. 2:8).

2. *Express your heart to God in prayer.* We need to go beyond merely reading prayers from devotional books alone. Prayers recited from a book are usually impersonal and seldom have much to do with where our hearts are with the Lord. They sound nice, but God wants to hear from *us.* Prayer is communion with God and He is pleased when we express our deepest desires to Him.

It also helps to expand our prayer vocabulary to include more specific and detailed expressions instead of just asking God to "bless" and "help" us. Habituation attacks through empty, vague words that don't really express what we want to say. It is sometimes difficult to open ourselves up to such intimate communication, but intimacy is what God is after.

3. *Avoid distractions.* Do you enjoy carrying on a conversation with a friend while the television is drowning you out? Do you like to exchange your innermost thoughts with someone who keeps leaving you to answer the telephone? Music, playing children, barking dogs and singing canaries can steal your attention away from the Lord and cause you to have an unproductive prayer time. If you can't remove the disturbance, remove yourself! God wants your attention, and you want His.

Perhaps you often find yourself distracted by a tendency to woolgather. If you have a wandering mind, it might be helpful to make a prayer list that will help you focus on one person or situation at a time. Above all, pray that the Holy Spirit will guide you as you learn to pray daily under His direction and control (Rom. 8:26, 27; Jude 20; Eph 6:18). The purpose of prayer is not just for you to talk to God; He wants to talk to you!

4. *Maintain a positive attitude in prayer.* Prayer should be more than lifting up our petitions to God, and begging Him to fulfill our requests. It should include praise and adoration for who He is and how He has proven Himself faithful in our lives (II Tim. 2:13). Prayer can become a depressing experience if we are simply restating our problems over and over, while losing sight of God's power and willingness to deal with them (Heb. 11:6). As we truly commit ourselves and our needs into His hands, with an attitude of thanksgiving, we can be assured of His ability to work for our best interests (Col. 4:2; I Pet. 5:7; Phil 4:4-6; I Thess. 5:18).